Dr. Maggie's
PHONICS
RESOURCE GUIDE

Written by
Margaret Allen, Ph.D.

Editor:
Joel Kupperstein

Illustrator:
Catherine Yuh

Designer:
Moonhee Pak

Project Director:
Carolea Williams

Table of Contents

Phonics: A New View

Welcome to the *Dr. Maggie's Phonics Readers* series and to the exciting challenge of helping children learn to read! This guide provides detailed ideas and activities for incorporating Dr. Maggie's Phonics Readers into your early-literacy curriculum. In this introduction, you'll learn about the background theory and purpose of these outstanding books and how this guide complements the books and completes a comprehensive, functional, and innovative phonics program.

Research confirms that for children to learn complex skills such as reading and writing they need to practice skills broken down into component parts. Practice makes perfect, it has often been said, but practice can also make permanent! Each time a child practices a skill, the access route for retrieving what was practiced becomes more and more automatic. Children need to practice skills they are learning; and they *want* to practice in order to "get good at it," as one first grader remarked. But practice needs to be provided in an engaging, meaningful format, rather than through rote memorization and meaningless drill. Dr. Maggie's Phonics Readers and this resource guide provide opportunities for children to practice skills in developmentally appropriate, engaging, and fun ways. Not only do children remember what makes sense to them, they remember what is fun to them. So, share with your students Dr. Maggie's Phonics Readers and the lessons provided in this guide and help them have fun learning to read!

The combination of the lessons in this guide and the 24 phonics readers constitutes a "new view" of phonics

instruction in three primary ways: it acknowledges children's recognition of sounds prior to their knowledge of letter/sound associations, it incorporates multimodal learning experiences, and its component phonics skills build from one book to the next in a natural literature context. Each of these features is contrasted with traditional phonics instruction in the following paragraphs.

Children's Sound Knowledge

In some traditional phonics programs, instruction does not consider children's awareness of sounds. Instead, children are first introduced to the letters of the alphabet and then to the sounds they represent. Teachers are encouraged to teach children all 26 letters and their sounds separately before they teach children how to blend the sounds and read words. Waiting through the long time period consumed by teaching isolated letters causes some children to see letter learning not as reading, but as an isolated and, perhaps, useless activity devoid of meaning or personal relevance. Unattached to meaningful reading activities, phonics instruction often stands alone, separate from "real" reading.

Dr. Maggie's Phonics Readers depart from this view of phonics. Teaching children sounds based on their knowledge of letters is unnatural. Because children learn to speak before they learn to read and write, moving from the sounds they hear and use to the letters associated with the sounds makes much better sense. In addition, waiting to learn all 26 letters of the alphabet before using this knowledge to read provides little immediate payoff for children. In the first book of the series, *I Spy*, children are presented a handful of the most commonly used consonants and one vowel. Children then practice with these letters, matching, blending, and using them to create and read words. Thoroughly learning this core set of letters facilitates children's learning of other consonants and vowels because they have "caught on" to what letters represent, how letters and sounds combine to make words, and how to blend letters and sounds to read words.

Multimodal Learning Experiences

Traditional phonics programs often call for children to reinforce their learning through a series of "fill-in" worksheets. While the validity of these worksheets is questionable, the more important issue is that the learning experience is neither engaging nor meaningful for children. This guide provides phonics activities that involve children in all three modalities—the visual, the auditory, and the kinesthetic. Teaching children basic phonics knowledge through "total body response" activities such as chanting, singing, physical movement, and active games motivates all children to participate in and benefit from your instruction.

Building Skills Book to Book

Phonics readers in traditional programs often contain contrived, stilted, unappealing text that makes little sense and seems to have little or no story line to which children can attach personal meaning. These books each focus on a separate skill in isolation rather than introduce the skill and integrate it with familiar elements. Thus, once again, children may perceive each piece of the reading puzzle as standing alone.

This 24-book series incorporates the most common phonics patterns young readers encounter. It begins with books focusing on only a few consonants and a vowel, and progresses to books with more advanced skills, such as word endings and two-syllable words. Each book blends skills from previous books with new skills that extend the reader's ability. This progression enables young readers to read successfully *while* they learn their letters and sounds rather than *after*. Simply being able to read an entire book independently makes a child hungry for more knowledge so that he or she can read even more books. In addition, the fun and familiar themes in combination with a variety of captivating illustration styles help children feel less like they are reading contrived instructional material and more like they are reading engaging, appealing literature.

Using This Guide

Each book in the series is accompanied by a section in this guide. The sections contain background information and step-by-step instructional ideas for taking children into, through, and beyond the skills and story of each book, as well as transitioning children from one book to the next. The following is a description of the headings found in each section.

Focus Skills

These are the new skills children need to be familiar with to read the book. Although these skills are the focus of the book, they are not the only skills practiced. Skills learned and practiced in previous books may also be necessary to read the book. Focus skills are listed on the readers themselves, both in the left margin of the front cover and in the scope and sequence chart on the inside back cover.

New Words

This list includes all words in the book that appear for the first time in the series. These words are divided into three categories:

Focus-Skill Words contain a new skill or sound introduced in the book.

Sight Words are among the most common words encountered in the English language. (See page 22 for a list of common sight words.)

Story Words are included to add flavor and interest to the story. They may or may not be decodable.

NEW WORDS

Focus-Skill Words
Jeff
stiff
stuff
all
ball
calls
doll
hill
Nell
well
Will
yell
mess
Russ
Tess

Sight Words
asks
one
this
what

Story Words
egg
make
says

Transition from Book to Book

Activities in this section are specifically designed to provide more practice with the skills learned in the previous book in the series, to introduce the focus skill of the new book, and to relate the new focus skill to those previously learned.

This section's activities are intended for implementation before children read the book. It includes the text for a rhythmic chant that coordinates with the story. The chants introduce some of the characters, themes, focus-skill words, sight words, and story words from the story. (Focus-skill words are bold in the text; sight and story words are underlined.) Coordinating activities help children practice reading the chant and make children's recognition of new words automatic. In addition, the steps of these activities include strategies for teaching phonemic awareness, letter/word awareness, and blending within the context of the chant and story. Many activities call for word or letter cards. Some of these cards appear in the reproducible section at the back of the book, while others must be prepared by hand. Focus-skill-, sight-, and story-word cards appear on reproducibles on the back of each chant chart (see below). Plan ahead so you will know what you must prepare for each lesson.

The chant charts included in the *Dr. Maggie's Phonics Readers* complete kit (CTP 2926) provide a convenient way to display these chants. You may wish to laminate these charts because many activities ask children to identify in writing words or letters in the chant. Laminating the charts and using "wipe-off" pens allows you to reuse the charts again and again. In addition, the backs of these charts have reproducible word cards for each story's focus-skill, sight, and story words. If you choose not to use the chant charts, a reproducible version of each chant is available at the end of its book's section. Create transparencies from these reproducibles so you can display the chants on an overhead projector. Other display options are to copy the chants onto chart paper or onto sentence strips for presentation in a pocket chart. You may also wish to give each student a copy of the chants to store in a poetry folder.

Note: If you use an overhead projector to lead children in reading text, point-track the words on the projection screen instead of on the projector itself. To children observing you tracking on the projector, you will appear to be reading from right to left. Work with the words on the screen to avoid this confusion.

 This section includes step-by-step suggestions for helping children read the book. The first few lessons are highly scaffolded, but later books move children toward taking over the

first reading of the book. The steps of the lessons call for several readings of the book—aloud by the teacher alone, aloud with children, silently by children independently, and aloud by children with partners. Research shows that children need an average of four to fourteen repetitions or exposures to words before they gain automaticity with those words. Research also shows that children need to read regularly to build fluency and skill as readers. Therefore, each of the repeated readings in the Read section is useful and worthwhile.

 This section provides ideas for studying the book's story line or focus skill, for blending sounds, and for practicing other "word work." Implement these activities after children have read the story several times and are familiar with the skills and story line. These activities are excellent for whole-group settings, small-group settings, or as independent learning centers.

 This section includes ideas for creating independent learning centers at which children can practice games, concepts, and skills learned during the Transition, Ready, and Read sections of the lesson.

Reproducibles and Bibliography
At the end of this guide are a section of reproducibles referenced within individual lessons and a bibliography that includes research information as well as titles of practical "teacher books" for extending ideas presented in this guide.

Teaching Strategies

PHONEMIC AWARENESS

(Look for this symbol to find phonemic awareness strategies throughout the lessons.)

For children to develop phonemic awareness (the awareness that each word is made up of specific sounds and the ability to play with sounds of language) they need repeated opportunities to listen to and play with language. Although each Ready section lesson plan in this guide includes phonemic-awareness teaching strategies, several other activities can be included in a lesson to further develop phonemic awareness. These activities include

- reading big books with rhyming words, alliteration, and repetition of rhythmic patterns.
- counting words in sentences.
- clapping syllables in words.
- reciting tongue twisters to play with alliteration.
- singing songs and chants to internalize the sounds of language and attend to the sounds that make up language.

(For specific, more detailed activities, consult the *Phonics* book from *Dr. Maggie's Play and Discover* series and *Phonemic Awareness: Playing with Sounds to Strengthen Beginning Reading Skills,* both published by Creative Teaching Press.)

LETTER/WORD AWARENESS

(Look for this symbol to find letter/word awareness strategies throughout the lessons.)

Activities that help children quickly recognize specific letters and words develop their automaticity and fluency with letter and word recognition. Research supports the need for basic skills to be mastered at the automaticity level so the reader can focus on the comprehension of what is read. Letter- and word-recognition teaching strategies are provided in each lesson's Ready section. The following activities may

be added to the lesson formats for additional practice during the lesson or at literacy-center time.

Feed the Monster: Draw a monster mask, and cut out eyes and a mouth. Place the mask on an overhead projector. Turn out the lights in the room. Place on the projector a row of letter cards or sight-word cards cut from a transparency. Pretend the "monster" is saying *Feed me a (letter or sight word).* Slowly move the letter or sight word through the monster's cut-out mouth and under the opaque part of the mask. It looks like the monster is eating the letter or word!

Rolling Letters: Write large capital letters on individual paper plates. Distribute a plate to each child. Call out a letter, and have the child with that letter's plate hold it up and turn it around and around. As the child turns the letter, have the class sing the following to the tune of "The Farmer in the Dell":

The ___ is rolling around. The ___ is rolling around.
As soon as the letter ___ stops, name something that starts with its sound.

Swat the Letter/Word: Obtain a flyswatter and a pair of tweezers. Place letter cards or word cards on a table or attach them to a wall. Call out a letter or word. Invite a child to swat the correct card with the flyswatter and pick it up with the tweezers. Challenge the child to then write the letter and use it in a word or write the word and use it in a sentence.

 ### BLENDING
(Look for this symbol to find blending strategies throughout the lessons.)

Since blending sounds is the core of reading, it is helpful to develop blending developmentally. Begin by teaching children to blend the onset or beginning sound to the rime or phonogram (e.g., *c* with *–at,* or *b* with *-ed).* Then, teach children to blend by having them segment each sound in the word and put the sounds together *(c-a-t* or *b-e-d).* Many lessons in this guide contain specific strategies for teaching blending in their Ready section. In addition, the following are fun ways to help children practice blending skills during any lesson.

Blending Slide: Draw a large slide on chart paper. Use nonpermanent tape to attach to the slide each letter in a word to be blended. Move the first letter down the slide, and say its sound. Then, slide the second letter into the first letter, and say the sounds together. Hold the second letter's sound, slide the third letter into the second letter, and blend the sounds together. This method, known as successive blending, is effective for children who have difficulty segmenting letters and blending their sounds.

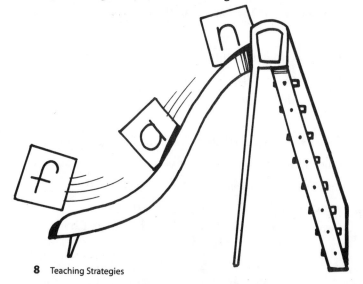

Link to Blend: Have children stand in front of the class and hold letter cards that spell a word to be blended. Ask each child to say the sound his or her letter makes. Then, have the first child say the sound, hold it, and link arms with the second child. Have the second child quickly say his or her sound and link arms with the third child, who quickly says his or her letter's sound. In this way, the three sounds are quickly linked or blended together to say the word.

Letter Chain: Write on individual small self-adhesive notes letters of a word to be blended. Have children link large paper clips together to make a chain. Stick each letter to a paper clip in the center of the chain. Point out that just as the paper clips link together to form a chain, the letters link together to form a word. Blend the letters to read the word. Repeat with other words.

 ### METACOGNITIVE THINKING
(Look for this symbol to find metacognitive coaching strategies throughout the lessons.)

In a systematic, explicit lesson, helping children know not only what they are doing, but how to verbalize why they are doing it is essential. This metacognitive thinking—thinking about a thought process—helps children retain strategies and understand how the learning process works. Many phonics readers' lesson plans provide in the Read section a metacognitive coaching strategy to help children think and talk about what they are doing as they decode, blend, sound out, and "solve" the text they are reading.

PHONICS

When children have phonemic awareness, have some letter awareness, and can recognize a core of consonants, they are ready for sound/letter pairing, or phonics. Phonics work should begin with basic elements, such as simple sound/letter matching, and move to more complex and subtle elements, such as vowel patterns and two-syllable words. This progression is reflected in this series' scope and sequence of skills.

Although more than one complex element, such as multiple letter combinations that represent a long vowel sound (e.g., *a-e, ai, ay*), may be a focus skill in a phonics reader, teach only one sound/letter pairing at a time, work with it until children are beginning to internalize it, and then teach other sound/letter pairings that make the same sound. (For example, teach *a-e,* then *ai,* then *ay,* when teaching the long *a* sound. Work with each combination before introducing Book 12, *Dave and Jane's Band.* After reading the book, review each sound/letter pairing that makes the long *a* sound.)

The new view of this phonics program recognizes the need to avoid a rule-laden program in which children memorize and then recall rules on demand to facilitate word recognition. Research argues against such a plan, acknowledging that the human brain functions as a pattern detector rather than as a rule memorizer and implementer. Oftentimes, the children rules are intended to help the most are the children who cannot remember the rules or who do not know how and when to use them. For these (and other) children, learning basic vowel patterns makes more sense.

Basic vowel patterns include

- the closed-vowel pattern (as in *cat, bed,* and *pig*).
- the long-vowel pattern in which the vowel ends the word (as in *me, hi,* and *go*).
- the silent *e* long-vowel pattern (as in *make, bite,* and *note*).
- the vowel-digraph pattern ("when two vowels go out walking, the first one does the talking" as in *boat* and *rain*).
- the vowel-diphthong pattern (as in *cow, toy,* and *oil*).
- the *r*-controlled pattern (as in *car, first,* and *turn*).
- the consonant-*le* pattern (as in *purple* and *apple*).

Jingles, chants, and stories that teach these patterns help children retrieve and implement them quickly.

WRITING

To encourage children to make use of their phonics skills, encourage them to write. Provide paper in a variety of colors, sizes, and shapes; many kinds of markers, pens, and pencils; and repeated opportunities to write, write, and write some more. Children reveal their level of phonics understanding when they invent spellings of words based on their understanding of how language works. (Be sure children spell sight words conventionally once they learn them.) As children move up the developmental ladder, their knowledge of phonics rises and they move closer to using conventional spellings. If forced to use conventional spelling too quickly, children may not develop the underlying knowledge of how language works and must rely on their memory alone when writing. Research reveals that the most successful plan encourages invented spelling at first and includes direct spelling instruction as children mature. In this way, children's ability to write and spell conventionally increases as their understanding increases, but their writing is not inhibited along the way.

Evaluation and Assessment

This resource includes four tools for assessing children's abilities and growth as they begin, work through, and complete the *Dr. Maggie's Phonics Readers* series. Administer to children each of the tools before beginning the series to establish their level of reading fluency and language awareness. Re-administer the tools periodically as children work through the stories and activities to measure their growth and to check that they retain skills taught with each reader. Finally, administer the assessment tools after children complete the series to confirm that they learned all the skills taught by the series. Keep completed copies of the tools in a separate file for each child so you can refer to previous assessments and measure children's progress.

Phonemic Awareness Inventory

This tool (pages 11–13) assesses children on five levels of phonemic awareness. It begins with simple concepts such as whole word discrimination and progresses to more complicated concepts such as phoneme deletion and phoneme substitution. This tool is administered **orally** and requires no reading on the child's part. It is designed to assess children's awareness of the *sounds* of language, not the *appearance* of language.

Letter Identification Checklist

This checklist (page 14) assesses children's recognition of capital letters. The letters appear on the checklist in the same order as in the scope and sequence of the *Dr. Maggie's Phonics Readers* series. Therefore, by the time children finish Book 7, the book in which the last remaining letter of the alphabet is introduced for the first time, they should achieve complete proficiency on this checklist.

Phonics Inventory

This inventory (pages 15–17) assesses children's ability to recognize and read letters and letter combinations in isolation. The order of the elements in this inventory matches the order of the elements in the scope and sequence of the series. If you choose to give this assessment before children begin the series, be prepared for their limited success. Use the results of this test as a benchmark by which children's progress can be measured. Administer the test periodically as children work through the series and compare the results to the original benchmark test. You may wish to administer this test after a child finishes each book to make sure that he or she has internalized the focus skill of that book.

Sight Words Inventory

The Sight Words Inventory (pages 18–20) is divided into three sections and assesses children's ownership of all sight words covered in the series. The first part covers sight words from books 1–5, the second covers sight words from books 6–13, and the third part covers sight words from books 14–24. Many of the words in this inventory appear in later books' Focus-Skill Word list, but because they are frequently occurring words and the books in which they first appear have not yet covered them as focus-skill words, they are considered sight words. Administer this inventory before students begin the series to assess their prior word knowledge. Then you may wish to reassess students after they complete each book, or after they complete the clusters of books into which the inventory is divided.

Student Name _____   Date _____

Phonemic-Awareness Inventory

D I R E C T I O N S

Give this inventory orally to each student.

Level

Whole Word Discrimination

Are these words the same? (Circle words child identifies correctly.)

fat–bat	red–rid	slip–slit
dip–hip	nut–nut	grip–grip
man–man	mat–map	flit–flip

Rhyming Words—Recognition

Do these words rhyme? (Circle words child identifies correctly.)

happy–sappy	boy–toy	sun–fun
sad–mad	girl–boy	play–game

Rhyming Words—Application

What word rhymes with _____? (Write child's responses on the lines.)

man _____   old _____   try _____

sun _____   play _____   skip _____

eat _____   book _____   scale _____

Syllable Counting

How many syllables do you hear in the word _____? (Write child's responses on the lines and circle those that are correct.)

ball _____   wagon _____   umbrella _____

elephant _____   hippopotamus _____   orangutan _____

Dr. Maggie's Phonics Resource Guide © 1999 Creative Teaching Press

Syllable Segmentation

I'll say a word, then you repeat it slowly. (Give examples: *cow-boy, ha-ppy, fu-nny.* Circle words to which child responds correctly.)

rainbow (rain-bow)   paper (pa-per)   scissors (sci-ssors)

doughnut (dough-nut)   basket (bas-ket)   butterfly (bu-tter-fly)

sidewalk (side-walk)   color (co-lor)   umbrella (um-bre-lla)

Oral Synthesis—Blending Speech Sounds

Listen and tell me the word I said. (Say each sound slowly. Circle words child identifies correctly.)

n-o	r-u-n	t-e-n	w-a-s	c-a-ke
s-ay	f-a-t	c-u-t	h-a-ve	w-e-n-t
m-e	s-i-t	m-o-p	s-ai-d	st-o-r-y

Approximation

Do you hear the /b/ sound at the beginning, middle, or end of _____? (Circle words child identifies correctly.)

big   robot   banana

tab   cabbage   crib

Phoneme Isolation

What sound do you hear _____? (Circle words child identifies correctly.)

First	Last	In the Middle
sun	water	feet
foot	buff	tub
yes	candy	lake
red	ten	pan

Dr. Maggie's Phonics Resource Guide © 1999 Creative Teaching Press

Level 4

Segmentation

Repeat each word slowly so I can hear each separate sound, like c-a-t. (Say a word and have child repeat it slowly, separating each phoneme. Circle each word child segments correctly.)

me	you	book
so	play	skip
man	old	scale

Level 5

Phoneme Deletion

Say the word _____, but leave off the _____. (Repeat, asking child to delete beginning or ending sounds. Circle each word to which child responds correctly.)

pop	dip	not	cub	fin
can	ten	tab	mop	set

Phoneme Substitution

Replace the first sound in _____ with _____. What is the new word? (Repeat each word twice, asking child to substitute middle and ending sounds. Circle words to which child responds correctly.)

pail	log	get
cat	tub	pop
pig	dice	jump

Student Name_____

Letter Identification Checklist

Check off each letter the child recognizes and names correctly.

Letter Name	Date #1	Date #2	Date #3	Date #4	Comments
M					
F					
S					
R					
H					
T					
C					
A					
P					
N					
B					
D					
G					
L					
J					
O					
W					
K					
I					
V					
Y					
U					
Z					
X					
E					
Q					

Phonics Inventory

(Part I)

DIRECTIONS

Point to each letter. Check those correctly identified. Ask child to tell what sound each letter or letters make.

Consonants	Date #1	Date #2	Date #3	Date #4	Comments
m					
t					
f					
h					
c					
r					
s					
p					
n					
b					
d					
g					
l					
j					
w					
k					
v					
y					
z					

Short Vowels	Date #1	Date #2	Date #3	Date #4	Comments
a					
o					
i					
u					
e					

Phonics Inventory

(Part 2)

······· **DIRECTIONS** ·······

Point to each letter or group of letters. Check those correctly identified.
Ask child to tell what sound each letter or letters make.

Special Sound/ Letter Teams	Date #1	Date #2	Date #3	Date #4	Comments
qu					
ck					

Consonant Digraphs	Date #1	Date #2	Date #3	Date #4	Comments
sh					
ch					
th					
wh					

Consonant Blends	Date #1	Date #2	Date #3	Date #4	Comments
tr					
gr					
dr					
cr					
fl					

Long Vowels	Date #1	Date #2	Date #3	Date #4	Comments
a					
e					
i					
o					
u					

Dr. Maggie's Phonics Resource Guide © 1999 Creative Teaching Press

Phonics Inventory

(Part 3)

DIRECTIONS

Point to each group of letters. Check those correctly identified.
Ask child to tell what sound each group of letters makes.

Vowel Digraphs	Date #1	Date #2	Date #3	Date #4	Comments
ay					
ai					
ee					
ea					
oa					

Diphthongs	Date #1	Date #2	Date #3	Date #4	Comments
oi					
oy					
ou					
ow					

Three-Letter Blends	Date #1	Date #2	Date #3	Date #4	Comments
str					
spl					
scr					

R-Controlled Vowels	Date #1	Date #2	Date #3	Date #4	Comments
ar					
er					
ir					
or					
ur					

Dr. Maggie's Phonics Resource Guide © 1999 Creative Teaching Press

Sight Words Inventory

Part 1 (Books 1–5)

········· **DIRECTIONS** ·········

Point to each word and ask the student to read it aloud. Mark each word read correctly.

Sight Word	Date #1	Date #2	Date #3	Date #4	Comments
a					
and					
I					
in					
no					
on					
the					
but					
have					
here					
of					
said					
to					
was					
is					
it					
new					
put					
so					
day					
gets					
you					
come					
plays					
then					

Dr. Maggie's Phonics Resource Guide © 1999 Creative Teaching Press

Sight Words Inventory

Part 2 (Books 6–13)

DIRECTIONS

Point to each word and ask the student to read it aloud. Mark each word read correctly.

Sight Word	Date #1	Date #2	Date #3	Date #4	Comments
do					
for					
off					
take					
we					
asks					
one					
this					
what					
likes					
sees					
things					
your					
now					
go					
look					
out					
time					
her					
into					
she					
they					
very					
sounds					

Dr. Maggie's Phonics Resource Guide © 1999 Creative Teaching Press

Sight Words Inventory

Part 3 (Books 14–24)

· · · · · · · · · · · · · · · · · · D I R E C T I O N S · · · · · · · · · · · · · · · · · ·

Point to each word and ask the student to read it aloud. Mark each word read correctly.

Sight Word	Date #1	Date #2	Date #3	Date #4	Comments
are					
good					
my					
from					
head					
little					
when					
does					
girls					
their					
learns					
move					
watch					
asked					
once					
open					
family					
great					
two					
began					
some					
talk					
want					
because					
school					
words					

Dr. Maggie's Phonics Resource Guide © 1999 Creative Teaching Press

Scope and Sequence

Bk.#	Title	Focus Skills
1	I Spy	m, f, s, r, h, t, c, short a
2	Hap and Cap	p, n, short a
3	Top Job, Mom!	b, d, g, l, j, short o
4	Pom-Pom's Big Win	w, k, short i
5	Pug's Hugs	v, y, short u
6	Jet It, Get It	z, x, short e
7	Click, Click	qu, ck
8	The ABC Bags	double f, l, and s
9	Sing-Song Sid	-ing, -ong, -ang
10	Draw and Share	consonant digraphs: sh, ch, th
11	Truck Tricks	consonant blends: tr, gr, dr, cr, fl
12	Dave and Jane's Band	long a: ay, a-e, ai
13	Pete's Street Beat	long e: ee, e-e, ea, ending e
14	Twice as Nice	long i: i-e
15	The Little Green Man Visits Pine Cone Cove	long o: o-e, oa, ow, ending o; -old
16	Mr. Noisy at the Dude Ranch	long u: u-e; /oi/ sound: oi, oy
17	Sad Sam and Blue Sue	oo, ue
18	Out to Gumball Pond	ew; ou as in *out*; ow as in *now*
19	Splish, Splash	3-letter blends: str, spl, scr
20	Barney Bear's Party	r-controlled vowels
21	The Rainy Day Band	contractions
22	Cat and Dog at the Circus	question words, soft c and g
23	Jo Jo in Outer Space	simple word endings: -er, -ed, -ly, -y
24	Riddle and Rhyme with Apron Annie	rhyming words, 2-syllable words

Dr. Maggie's Phonics Resource Guide © 1999 Creative Teaching Press

Common Sight Words

a	from	me	their
about	get	more	them
all	gets	move	then
am	girl	my	there
an	go	new	they
and	goes	no	thing
are	going	not	this
as	good	now	time
asked	great	of	to
asks	had	off	two
at	has	on	up
be	have	once	use
because	he	one	very
been	head	open	want
began	her	or	was
blue	here	out	watch
but	his	play	we
by	how	please	went
call	I	put	were
can	if	said	what
care	in	saw	when
come	into	school	where
could	is	see	which
day	it	she	who
did	learn	so	will
do	like	some	with
does	little	sound	words
down	long	take	yellow
each	look	talk	yes
family	made	than	you
first	make	that	your
for	many	the	

Dr. Maggie's Phonics Resource Guide © 1999 Creative Teaching Press

1 I Spy

FOCUS SKILLS m, f, s, r, h, t, c, short a

Prior to beginning the first book in the series there are several concepts about print with which children should be familiar.

1 They should understand the connection between thought, oral language, and written language. As children learn to speak, they realize that their thoughts can be communicated through language. As they learn to read, they realize that their thoughts can be written down and understood by others, providing those others know how to read. Children recognize the value of reading when they understand that writing is "speaking on paper" and is a way to communicate about experiences. For this reason, children's earliest literacy activities should invite them to communicate about their own personal experiences.

2 They should understand that print is all around them. Surrounding children with a print-rich environment helps them recognize the value of being able to comprehend the printed word, in other words, to read.

3 Children should understand the mechanics of print, including the ideas that we read from left to right and that sentences begin with capital letters and end with punctuation.

4 Children need to understand the alphabetic principle—the idea that the sounds of oral language map onto the symbols that make up written language. Once children understand that the squiggly black lines on a page represent sounds and words, they can begin to unlock the alphabetic principle. The primary goal of this and any phonics program is to give children the key to unlocking the alphabetic principle.

Assess how well children understand these concepts and provide them with opportunities to explore them through environmental print, through listening to stories, and through oral discussion. When children have a grasp of these concepts, they are ready to learn their first set of focus skills and begin Book 1.

NEW WORDS

Focus-Skill Words

cat

fat

hat

mat

rat

scat

Sight Words

a

and

I

in

no

on

the

Story Words

oh

spy

READY

Prior to this lesson, children should have been introduced to the letters and corresponding sounds of *m, f, s, r, h, t, c,* and short *a.*

Book 1 Rhythmic Chant
The Fat Cat in the Hat
(to the tune of "The Farmer in the Dell")

The **fat cat** in the **hat.**
The **fat cat** in the **hat.**
The **fat cat** in the **hat**
and the **rat**
on a **mat.**
Scat!

(Chant reproducible on page 28)

1 Read *The Fat Cat in the Hat* to children. Point to each word, and read slowly as the children follow top to bottom, left to right.

2 Read the chant again rhythmically, pointing to each word. Have children clap a steady beat as you read.

3 Sing the chant to the tune of "The Farmer in the Dell."

4 Sing the chant again with children participating.

5 Have children match word cards to words in the chant, line by line.

6 Place the sight-word cards in a pocket chart. Have children read the sight words *the, in, and, on,* and *a.*

7 Place the focus-skill-word cards in the pocket chart. Ask *What do you notice about these words? Listen carefully as I say them.* Help children discover that the words *fat, cat, hat, rat, mat,* and *scat*

have a common phonogram in them *(-at),* but each word starts with a different letter.

8 **Phonemic Awareness Strategy:** Ask children *What sound do you hear at the beginning of these words?* Say *fat, cat, hat, rat,* and *mat* slowly. Have children respond by saying the corresponding sound.

9 **Letter/Word Awareness Strategy:** Again display the focus-skill-word cards. Highlight the letters *c, f, h, m,* and *r* on the word cards or write the words on the board using a different color for each beginning sound and the same color each time for the *-at* phonogram. Have children look at and name each letter of the word by having them spell the word, beginning letter first followed by the letters in the phonogram.

10 **Blending Strategy:** Have children break the words into chunks as they read them aloud—*f- at, fat; c- at, cat; h- at, hat; r- at, rat; m- at, mat.* Have children extend their left arm as they say the beginning sound, extend their right arm when they say the phonogram, and pull both arms back as they read the word.

11 Write the word *cat* on the board. Have children say each letter and then identify the word. Write an *s* and have children identify the letter and its sound. Add *s* to the beginning of the word *cat* and help children read *scat*.

12 Point-track and sing *The Fat Cat in the Hat* once more.

When children have had sufficient practice with the rhythmic chant; recognize most new sight words; and seem confident with the suggested phonemic awareness, letter/word awareness, and blending activities, they are ready to read Book 1.

1 Hold up *I Spy*. Encourage children to make predictions about the book by asking open-ended questions such as *What do you notice on the front cover of our book?* and *What do you think our story will be about?* Identify the title, author, and illustrator.

2 Read the story as children listen. Ask children if they have ever played the game "Oh My, I Spy." Tell children they will play the game later. Then, hold up the *spy* and *oh* word cards and identify the words for the children.

3 **Metacognitive Coaching Strategy:** Distribute children's books. Read the story as children follow word by word. Pause frequently on words with the *-at* phonogram to demonstrate sounding them out. Say *This word starts with* c. *That's a /k/ sound. It has* -at *in it. That's /at/. So the word is* c-at, cat! *The word is* cat.

4 Read on and call children's attention to the story words *spy* and *oh*.

5 Have children read the story independently page by page in a soft voice. Move around the group, listen, and observe children's progress as they decode words and recognize the sight words.

6 Have children pair off and read simultaneously to each other page by page. Move among the pairs to listen to their reading.

7 Again, have children read independently in a low voice. Move about and assess their progress.

Letter/Word Recognition

After reading, review focus-skill letters, sounds, and words (as well as concepts of print) by playing a game of "Oh My, I Spy" with the children. Place pre-made cards with all focus-skill letters, focus-skill words, sight words, and story words around the room on top of, above, below, over, under, in between, to the left of, or to the right of objects in the room.

To begin the game, chant rhythmically
Oh my, I spy
a letter card with t.
Tell me, tell me, where do I spy t?

Have children respond rhythmically
Oh my, you spy
a letter card with t.
I'll tell, I'll tell, where you can find t.
It is _____!

Then chant
Oh my, I spy
a word card with and.
Tell me, tell me, where do I spy and?

Have children respond rhythmically
Oh my, you spy
a word card with and.
I'll tell, I'll tell, where you can find and.
It is _____!

Play until children have reviewed all focus-skill-letter cards and their corresponding sounds and as many focus-skill words, sight words, and story words as time will allow.

Blending Phonograms

Write the letters *a* and *t* on two connected red linking cubes. Read them to the children. Write each of the letters *c, f, h, m, r,* and *s* on cubes of another color. Hold up one letter at a time, say its sound, say the phonogram sound, link the letter and the phonogram together, and blend the beginning sound onto the phonogram. Have children extend their left arm as they say the initial sound, extend their right arm as they say the phonogram, and pull both arms back as they read the whole word.

Blending Sounds

Write on individual 1"-wide (2.5 cm) elastic strips the words *fat, mat, rat, sat, hat, cat,* and *scat.* Stretch out each word strip. As you stretch the word, say it slowly, segmenting each sound. As you release the stretched word, blend it back together, holding each sound until the next sound is voiced. (This is known as successive blending.)

REINFORCE

Pocket Chart Center

Place a pocket chart, a copy of the rhythmic chant (*The Fat Cat in the Hat*), and a copy of *I Spy* in the pocket chart center. Make a set of letter cards, focus-skill-word cards, sight-word cards, and story-word cards. Punch a hole in each card, and place each set of cards on a different metal ring. Invite children to work with the cards independently or with a partner to retell parts of the story, to match the cards to words in the book, or to retell or match words to the chant. Children can also play "Read-a-Ring" by simply reading all the letter or word cards on a ring to a partner.

Song and Poem Center

Place in a box labeled *Song Box* a hard copy of the rhythmic chant. Invite children to point-track the words and sing the chant to the tune of "The Farmer in the Dell."

Overhead Projector Center

Place a transparency copy of the rhythmic chant in the overhead projector center. Have children project the chant on the wall and "walk the words," tapping each word on the wall as they read it. Have children use transparency pens to circle focus-skill words, box off sight words, underline story words, or trace target letters.

Library Center

Place in the library center copies of *I Spy* for children to read and reread alone, to a partner, to an older "book buddy," or to a visiting parent.

Alphabet/Word Study Center

Place the linking cubes and the elastic word strips from the Review section in the center for children to manipulate and review independently.

The Fat Cat in the Hat

(to the tune of "The Farmer in the Dell")

The fat cat in the hat.

The fat cat in the hat.

The fat cat in the hat

and the rat

on a mat.

Scat!

BOOK
2 Hap and Cap

FOCUS SKILLS p, n, short a

TRANSITION FROM BOOK 1 TO BOOK 2

Going on a Letter/Word Hunt
Randomly place magnetic letters *a, c, f, h, m, n, p, r, s,* and *t* on an overhead projector and project them on a wall. Place letter cards for these same letters in a pile. Ask a child volunteer to hold a large magnifying glass. Have children repeat after you, echo-chant style.

Teacher:
Going on a letter hunt.
Ooooh, look-eee! (Select a letter card.)
What is it?
It's a(n) _____. (Identify the letter.)
Can you find one?
Can I find one?
Let's start looking.
Here we go.

Children:
Going on a letter hunt.
Ooooh, look-eee!
What is it?
It's a(n) _____.
Can you find one?
Can I find one?
Let's start looking.
Here we go.

Hold the volunteer's hand, and help him or her pretend to use the magnifying glass to spot the letter you identified projected on the wall. Identify it by having the volunteer match the letter card to the one on the wall.

Continue the game for several turns and then repeat it using focus-skill words and sight words from Book 1. (Instead of using magnetic letters, write these words on scraps of transparency film and scatter them randomly on the overhead projector.) Project the words onto the wall or a large sheet of paper. Write each word on a corresponding card and place it facedown in a pile. Begin the game again, but instead of going on a Letter Hunt, go on a Word Hunt. Play until children have had an opportunity to review all focus-skill letters and sounds and as many words as time allows.

NEW WORDS

Focus-Skill Words
c**a**n
pan
r**a**n
Cap
Hap
Pam
r**a**p
t**a**p
at
h**a**m
m**a**t

Sight Words
but
have
here
of
said
to
was

Story Word
fast

READY

Prior to this lesson, children should have been working with activities suggested for Book 1 to build phonemic and letter/sound awareness. These activities should have been extended to introduce *p, n,* and short *a* letter/sound correspondences.

Book 2 Rhythmic Chant
Here, Hap and Cap

"<u>Here</u>, **Hap** and **Cap**.
<u>Here</u>," <u>said</u> **Pam**.
"I <u>have</u>, I <u>have</u>,
I <u>have</u> **ham**."

"<u>Here</u>, **Hap** and **Cap**.
<u>Here</u>," <u>said</u> **Pam**.
"A **can** <u>of</u>, a **can** <u>of</u>,
a **can** <u>of</u> **ham!**"

"<u>Fast</u> <u>to</u> the **pan**.
<u>Fast</u> <u>to</u> the **pan**.
<u>Fast</u> <u>to</u> the **pan** <u>of</u> **ham**,"
<u>said</u> **Pam**.

(Chant reproducible on page 34)

❶ Read *Here, Hap and Cap* to the children. Point to each word, and read slowly as children follow top to bottom, left to right.

❷ Set a beat for the chant by clapping two times on your legs and then clapping your hands together once. (Legs, legs, hands! Legs, legs, hands!) Emphasize the hands-together clap so that it creates a pattern of 1, 2, 3, 1, 2, 3. Once the rhythmic accompaniment is established, read the chant again rhythmically to the beat.

❸ Have the children read the chant rhythmically with you as you point to the words.

❹ If you are using the chant on an overhead transparency, place a sheet of paper on the wall and trace a sight word or story word on it. If you are using a chart of the chant, place a blank transparency sheet over the chart and trace a sight word or story word onto the blank transparency. Continue the process until all sight words have been traced, each one in a different color.

❺ Have children read each sight and story word and then reverse the process by matching the words back to the chant.

❻ Display all sight and story words, and have children read them aloud.

❼ Write the words *Hap, Cap, rap,* and *tap* on individual index cards or sentence strips. With children watching, trace the *ap* in each word with a red marker. Have volunteers hold the cards. Ask children to describe what they notice about the four words. (All four words belong to the -ap word family.) Read each word aloud and have children repeat it.

8 Repeat the procedure for the words *can, pan,* and *ran; at* and *mat;* and *ham* and *Pam.*

9 Place all focus-skill-word cards in a pocket chart in word-family rows. Help children discover that each family of words has a common phonogram but each word in the family starts with a different letter.

10 **Phonemic Awareness Strategy:**
Tell children *I am going to say two words. If the words begin with the same sound, hold both of your arms up in the air. If the words do not begin with the same sound, hold up your arms but cross them to make a big X. Ready? Cat/can. Ham/ran. Pam/pan. Ran/rat.*

11 **Letter/Word Awareness Strategy:**
Place magnetic letters *a, C, H, n, p, r,* and *t* on a magnetic board. Display the -ap phonogram. Add *H* to it, and have children spell *Hap.* Remove *H* and ask children what is needed to write *Cap.* Add *C* to *ap,* and read the word. Remove *C* and ask what is needed to write *rap, tap,* or *nap.* Mix up the letters on the magnetic board, and have children identify *a, C, H, n, p, r,* and *t.*

12 **Blending Strategy:** Have children read the words *Hap, Cap, rap, tap,* and *nap.* Have children extend their left arm for the beginning sound, extend their right arm for the phonogram, and pull both arms back in for the whole word. (This is a review of the process used in Book 1 for phonogram blending practice.)

13 Display the chart or transparency of *Here, Hap and Cap.* Once again, point-track and read rhythmically as children join in.

When children have had sufficient practice with the rhythmic chant; recognize most new sight words; and seem confident with the suggested phonemic awareness, letter/word awareness, and blending activities, they are ready to read Book 2.

1 Hold up *Hap and Cap.* Ask open-ended questions such as *What do you notice on the front cover of our book?* and *What do you think our story will be about?* Identify the title, author, and illustrator.

2 **Metacognitive Coaching Strategy:**
Read the story as children listen. Pause once or twice to read a word with the -ap phonogram (e.g., *Hap, Cap, rap, tap*) as if "stumped" by it. Think out loud by saying the beginning letter and its sound. Recognize and read the -ap phonogram. Blend them together for the children. Reread the sentence, saying the word correctly in context, and move on.

3 After reading, ask children if they have pets. Ask them if their pets come when they are called.

4 Distribute children's books. Read the story aloud as children follow. Call children's attention to the sight words *was* and *but*. These two words are new and are not in the chant *Here, Hap and Cap*.

5 Have children "pair off" or "square off" (groups of two or four) and read independently in a soft voice. Move among the children as they read. Listen and observe their progress with decoding words and recognizing the sight words.

6 Have children read "verse-choir" style. Ask them to read with you simultaneously, following your lead. Notice which children are reading with you, which are reading at a slower pace, and which are not reading at all. Remind children that a verse choir works only when everyone reads together!

7 Have children read independently in a low voice. Move among them as they read to assess their progress.

Blending Phonograms

Write the letters *a* and *p* on red linking cubes. Link them, and read the phonogram to children. Write each of the letters *c, f, h, m, n, r,* and *s* on cubes of another color. Hold up one letter at a time, say its sound, say the phonogram sound, link the letter to the phonogram, and blend the beginning sound onto the phonogram. Have children extend their left arm on the initial sound, extend their right arm on the phonogram, and pull both arms back as they read the whole word.

The Blending Tray Game

Place Alphabet Cards (pages 141–143) for *f, m, n, r,* and *s* in one small section of a TV-dinner tray with three compartments, two small and one large. Place six *a* cards in the other small section. Select a consonant and say its sound, holding the sound as you place the card in the tray's large section. Select an *a* and, as you pick it up and place it in the large section next to the consonant, blend the consonant's sound into the *a*'s sound. After you model this once, have children join in a couple of times. Then, have volunteers finish the game.

Overhead Projector Center

Place a transparency of the rhythmic chant in the overhead projector center. Have children project the chant on the wall, quietly initiate the rhythmic clapping accompaniment, and read the chant. Children can place sheets of paper on the projected chant and trace their own copies of focus-skill and sight words.

Pocket Chart Center

Place a copy of the rhythmic chant *(Here, Hap and Cap)*, a collection of pointers, and a copy of *Hap and Cap* in the pocket chart center. Invite children to point-track and read the words of the chant for reading reinforcement and practice. As one child leads the pocket chart reading, other children can follow and read in the small book.

Song and Poem Center

Place a copy of the rhythmic chant in a song box. Place rhythm band instruments in another box. Have children play in groups of three. As one child points to the words, a second child plays the chant's accompaniment, and the third child reads the rhythmic chant.

Library Center

Place in the library center copies of the book *Hap and Cap* for children to read and reread alone, to a partner, to an older book buddy, or to a visiting parent.

Alphabet/Word Study Center

Place the linking cubes and the blending tray from the Review section in the center for children to manipulate and review independently.

Here, Hap and Cap

"Here, Hap and Cap.
Here," said Pam.
"I have, I have,
I have ham."

"Here, Hap and Cap.
Here," said Pam.
"A can of, a can of,
a can of ham!"

"Fast to the pan.
Fast to the pan.
Fast to the pan of ham,"
said Pam.

Dr. Maggie's Phonics Resource Guide © 1999 Creative Teaching Press

3 Top Job, Mom!

FOCUS SKILLS b, d, g, l, j, short o

TRANSITION FROM BOOK 2 TO BOOK 3

Sift a Letter/Sift a Word

Place in a pan cards containing the letters *a, b, c, d, f, g, h, j, l, m, n, o, p, r, s,* and *t* and the sight words from Books 1 and 2. Cover the cards with 2–3" (5–7.5 cm) of rice, sand, or clean cat litter. Divide the class into small groups, and have each group use a slotted spoon or cat litter scoop to sift through the loose material to reveal letter and word cards. Have children identify the letters and say the corresponding sound or read the words on the cards to other children in the group. Play until children have had an opportunity to review all focus-skill letters and their corresponding sounds as well as the sight words from Books 1 and 2.

NEW WORDS

Focus-Skill Words

bad

A**l**

got

job

lot

cot

hot

M**o**m

n**o**t

P**o**p

s**to**p

T**o**m

t**o**p

Sight Words

is

it

new

put

so

Story Words

blew

cool

uh

yes

Prior to this lesson, children should have been working with activities suggested for Book 2 to build phonemic and letter/sound awareness. These activities should have been extended to introduce *b, d, g, l, j,* and short *o* letter/sound correspondences.

Book 3 Rhythmic Chant
It Got So Hot

It **got** so **hot.**
It **got** so **hot.**
It **got** so **hot,**
but I am **not.**

The new fan blew.
The new fan blew.
The new fan blew,
so I am cool.

It is **hot,**
but I am **not.**
I am cool.
Yes! Cool, cool, cool!

(Chant reproducible on page 39)

❶ Read *It Got So Hot* to the children. Point to each word, and read slowly as children follow top to bottom, left to right.

❷ Beat a drum in a slow 1-2, 1-2 beat. Read the chant, emphasizing the beat. (For example, *It got so hot. It got so hot. It got so hot, but I am not.*)
   1   2   1   2   1   2   1   2

❸ Beat the drum, and read the chant again with the children, chanting as you point to the words.

❹ Have children play the beat on their legs. Read the chant again with the children as they play the beat and you point to the words.

❺ Write *It, got, so, hot, but, I, am,* and *not* on individual large index cards. Punch holes in the cards, and string yarn through the holes to create "necklaces." Invite eight volunteers to each wear one card. Have the children wearing the cards crouch down in a row in front of the group. Read the first verse of the chant as a group, and have each child wearing a necklace stand up when his or her word is read and sit down on the next word. Have the child remain sitting until his or her word is read again. Continue playing this game (called "Be the Words") verse by verse until all three verses are read.

6 **Phonemic Awareness Strategy:**
Tell children *Let's play a game called "Listen for the Rhyme." I will read the first verse of the chant to you. Whenever you hear a word that rhymes with* pot, *hold your hands up behind your ears like you are listening for the rhyme. Ready?* Read the first verse slowly, and observe which children indicate the signal for the rhyming words *got, hot,* and *not.*

7 **Letter/Word Awareness Strategy:**
Display magnetic letters on a magnetic board. Display the *-ot* phonogram. Add *g* to it, and have children spell *got.* Remove *g* and ask children what is needed to write *pot.* Remove *p* and ask what is needed to spell *hot, not, dot, jot,* and *lot.* Mix up the letters on the magnetic board, and have children identify *d, g, h, j, l, n, o, p,* and *t.*

8 **Blending Strategy:** Have children read the words *got, pot, hot, not, dot, jot,* and *lot.* Have children extend their left arm for the beginning sound, extend their right arm for the phonogram, and pull both arms back in for the whole word. (This is a review of the process used in Books 1 and 2 for phonogram blending practice.)

9 Display the chart or transparency of *It Got So Hot.* Point-track and read rhythmically as children join in.

READ

When children have had sufficient practice with the rhythmic chant; recognize most new sight words; and seem confident with the suggested phonemic, letter/word awareness, and blending activities, they are ready to read Book 3.

1 Hold up *Top Job, Mom!* Ask open-ended questions such as *What do you notice on the front cover of our book?* and *What do you think our story will be about?* Identify the title, author, and illustrator of the book.

2 **Metacognitive Coaching Strategy:**
Read the story as children listen. Pause on one or two *-ot* phonogram words and on the word *Mom.* Think aloud how to decode the words by saying the beginning letter and its sound and then recognizing and reading the phonogram. Blend aloud the beginning sound and the *-ot* phonogram for the children. When reading *Mom,* notice (aloud) that the phonogram has changed. Blend the beginning sound and the new phonogram to correctly read the word. For each word during the thinking-aloud process, reread the sentence and correctly identify the word in context.

3 After reading, ask children if they remember a hot day. Ask them to share how they felt and what they did to cool off.

4 Distribute children's books. Read the story as children follow page by page. Call children's attention to the sight word *put.* This word is new and is not in the rhythmic chant.

5 Read again slowly, and have children read with you.

6 Have children pair off and read simultaneously in a soft voice to each other. Move among the pairs.

Listen and observe their progress with decoding words and recognizing sight words.

7 Have children reread the story simultaneously with you. Observe each child's pace and fluency to assess progress.

Blending Phonograms

Draw on chart paper a large tree labeled *Word Family Tree.* Write *-op* on the trunk. On each branch of the tree, write a nonsense word or a real word using the focus-skill letters *b, d, g, j,* and *l* (e.g., *bop, dop, gop, jop, lop*). Ask children to blend these words as *b-op, d-op, g-op, j-op,* and *l-op* as they read. Ask children *Are these real words or make-believe words?* Now add other words to the family tree. Write *Pop, top,* and *stop,* and have children blend the beginning letter to the phonogram. Ask if these are real or pretend words.

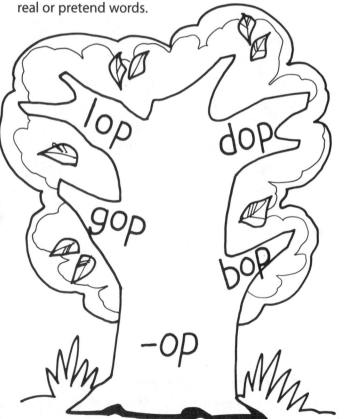

The Blending Tray Game

Place Alphabet Cards (pages 141–143) for *b, d, g, j,* and *l* in one small section of a TV-dinner tray. Place three *a* cards and three *o* cards in the other small section. Select a consonant and say its sound, holding the sound as you place the card in the tray's large section. Select an *a* or an *o* from the tray and place it in the large section next to the consonant. Blend the consonant's sound into the short vowel's sound. After you model this once, have children join in to finish the game together.

Chart Center

Place a copy of the rhythmic chant *(It Got So Hot)* and the word-card necklaces from "Be the Words" (see the Ready section) in the chart center. Have one child lead the chant while other children play "Be the Words" to practice recognition of the new sight words.

Overhead Projector Center

Place the magnetic letters used in the Ready section, Step 7, in the overhead projector center. Invite children to manipulate them and display them on the wall to spell and read *-ot* word-family words.

Library Center

Place in the library center copies of the book *Top Job, Mom!* for children to read alone, to a partner, to an older book buddy, or to a visiting parent.

Alphabet/Word Study Center

Place in the center the letter cards and the blending tray from the Review section so children can independently practice blending words with short *a* and short *o.*

It Got So Hot

It got so hot.
It got so hot.
It got so hot,
but I am not.

The new fan blew.
The new fan blew.
The new fan blew,
so I am cool.

It is hot,
but I am not.
I am cool.
Yes! Cool, cool, cool!

Pom-Pom's Big Win

FOCUS SKILLS w, k, short i

TRANSITION FROM BOOK 3 TO BOOK 4

3-D to Me!
Create and place transparency cards for letters *a, b, c, d, f, g, h, j, l, m, n, o, p, r, s,* and *t* (add *w, k,* and *i* later) on an overhead projector. Staple a white paper plate to a tongue depressor. Dim the classroom lights. Project the letter cards, and dramatically call out a letter in this manner: *3-D to me. Show me* g! Hold the "letter-catcher" plate in front of that letter on the projected image. Move the letter catcher away from the screen, making sure the letter's image is still on the plate. As you get closer to the projector and farther from the wall, the letter seems to "jump off" the wall, mesmerizing and delighting the children! After you have modeled this several times, allow student volunteers to make the letters jump off the wall. Play until children have had an opportunity to review all focus-skill letters and corresponding sounds. Then, place transparency scraps with the Book 4 sight words written on them on the overhead. Play the game again, but this time call out a word instead of a letter. Play until all letters and words have been reviewed.

NEW WORDS

Focus-Skill Words

win

wins

Kip

big

grin

hits

is

it

sit

sits

spins

Sight Words

day

gets

you

Story Words

blue

pets

ribbon

today

toy

READY

Prior to this lesson, children should have been working with activities suggested for Book 3 to build phonemic and letter/sound awareness. These activities should have been extended to introduce *w*, *k*, and short *i* letter/sound correspondences.

Book 4 Rhythmic Chant
Today Is the Day
(to the tune of "Did You Ever See a Lassie?")

<u>Today</u> **is** the <u>day</u>,
the <u>day</u>, the <u>day</u>.
<u>Today</u> **is** the <u>day</u>,
the <u>day</u> Pom-Pom **wins.**

<u>Today</u> Pom-Pom **sits,**
and **sits,** and **hits.**
<u>Today</u> Pom-Pom **spins.**
<u>Today</u> Pom-Pom **wins!**

(Chant reproducible on page 44)

❶ Read *Today Is the Day* to the children. Point to each word, and read slowly as children follow top to bottom, left to right.

❷ Read the chant again rhythmically, pointing to each word. Have children clap a steady beat as you read.

❸ Sing the chant to the tune of "Did You Ever See a Lassie?"

❹ Sing the chant again with children participating.

❺ Place all sight-word cards in a pocket chart. Have children read aloud the words *today* and *day*.

❻ Have children match word cards to words in the chant, line by line.

❼ Place all focus-skill-word cards in the pocket chart. Say *What do you notice about* wins *and* spins? *About* sits *and* hits? *About the name* Pom-Pom? Through questioning and coaching, help children discover the common phonograms present *(-in* and *-it)* and that the cat's name rhymes with *Mom* and *Tom* (from Book 3) and belongs in the *-om* word family.

8 **Phonemic Awareness Strategy:**
Ask children to listen to pairs of words such as *win/tan, mitt/mat, Kip/tap,* and *cat/can.* Ask them where the words sound alike, at the beginning of the word or at the end.

9 **Letter/Word Awareness Strategy:**
Display magnetic letters on a magnetic board. Display the *-in* phonogram. Add *w* to it, and have children read the word *win.* Remove *w* and ask children what is needed to spell *tin.* Remove *t* and ask what is needed to spell *fin, pin, bin, kin, grin,* and *spin.* Mix up the letters on the magnetic board, and have children identify *b, f, g, i, k, p, r, s,* and *w.*

10 **Blending Strategy:** Have children read the words *bin, fin, kin, pin, tin, grin,* and *spin.* Have them extend their left arm as they say the beginning sound(s), extend their right arm as they say the phonogram, and pull both arms back in as they read the word. (This is a review of the process used in previous books for phonogram blending practice.)

11 Display the chart or transparency of *Today Is the Day.* Point-track and read the chant rhythmically as children join in.

When children have had sufficient practice with the rhythmic chant; recognize most new sight words; and seem confident with the suggested phonemic, letter/word awareness, and blending activities, they are ready to read Book 4.

1 Hold up *Pom-Pom's Big Win.* Ask open-ended questions such as *What do you notice on the front cover of our book?* and *What do you think our story will be about?* Identify the title, author, and illustrator.

2 **Metacognitive Coaching Strategy:** Read the story as children listen. Pause on the word *sit.* Think aloud how to decode the word. Say the beginning letter and its sound, and then recognize and read the phonogram. Blend aloud the beginning sound and the *-it* phonogram. Read the entire word. Go back and read the word in context, and then continue reading the book. Tape-record yourself reading the book (including your modeling of the decoding process for *sit*). Keep this tape for later use in a listening center.

3 Distribute children's books. Read the story as children follow page by page. Call children's attention to the sight and story words *gets, you,* and *blue.* These words are new to the series and are not in the rhythmic chant.

4 Read the book again slowly, and have the children read with you.

5 Have the children read independently in a soft voice. Move around the group as children read. Listen and observe their progress with decoding words and recognizing sight words.

6 Have children reread the story simultaneously with you. Observe each child's pace and fluency to assess progress.

The Blending Tray Game
Place Alphabet Cards (pages 141–143) for *b, d, g, j, k, l,* and *w* in one small section of a TV-dinner tray. Place two *a* cards, two *o* cards, and three *i* cards in the other small section. Select a consonant and say its sound, holding the sound as you place the card in the tray's large section. Select a vowel card. As you pick it up and place it in the large section next to the

consonant, blend the consonant's sound into the short vowel's sound. After you model this once, have children join in to finish the game together.

Blue Ribbon Words

Draw on chart paper or poster board a large blue ribbon, and cut it out. Write -it at the top of the ribbon. Below, write *fit, hit, kit, lit, pit, sit,* and *wit.* Trace in red the phonogram -it in each word. Trace the beginning letter of each word (the "onset") in a different color. Help children read the words by having them stand up as they say the onset of each word, sit down as they say the -it phonogram, and clap their hands as they read the whole word. (For example, stand up on *f,* sit down on *it,* and clap on *fit.*)

Chart Center

Place in the chart center a copy of the rhythmic chant *(Today Is the Day)* and word-card necklaces similar to those in the "Be the Words" game (see Book 3's Ready section, Step 5). Have one child lead the chant while other children play "Be the Words" to practice recognition of new sight words.

Overhead Projector Center

Place the magnetic letters used in the Ready section, Step 9, in the overhead projector center. Have children manipulate them and display them on the wall to spell and read -ot word-family words.

Listening Center

Place in the listening center copies of *Pom-Pom's Big Win* and the tape made during your introductory reading of the book for children to follow along and read. You may also wish to include a taped reading of the story in which there are no metacognitive pauses.

Today Is the Day

(to the tune of "Did You Ever See a Lassie?")

Today is the day,
the day, the day.
Today is the day,
the day Pom-Pom wins.

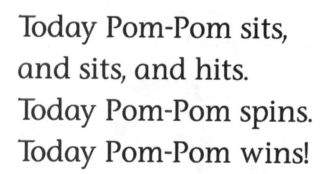

Today Pom-Pom sits,
and sits, and hits.
Today Pom-Pom spins.
Today Pom-Pom wins!

5 Pug's Hugs

FOCUS SKILLS v, y, short u

TRANSITION FROM BOOK 4 TO BOOK 5

Name That Letter/Word

Divide the class into groups of four, five, or six. Have each group sit in a circle, and place letter cards *a, b, c, d, f, g, h, j, k, l, m, n, o, p, r, s, t, v, w,* and *y* in a pile in the center of each circle. Designate a leader in each group. On a signal (ring a bell or play music), have the leader draw a card from the pile and start passing it from child to child around the circle until the music stops or the bell rings again. Invite the child in each circle holding the card to name the letter. After the groups have practiced with letters, replace the letter cards with cards containing the sight words from Books 1–4.

NEW WORDS

Focus-Skill Words

van

yard

yes

b**u**g

b**u**t

c**u**p

h**u**gs

j**u**mps

P**u**g

p**u**p

r**u**g

t**u**gs

up

Sight Words

come

plays

then

Story Words

den

licks

pulls

READY

Prior to this lesson, children should have been working with activities suggested for Book 4 to build phonemic and letter/sound awareness. These activities should have been extended to introduce *v*, *y*, and short *u* letter/sound correspondences.

Book 5 Rhythmic Chant
Pug the Pup
(to the tune of "London Bridge Is Falling Down")

Pug the **pup**
<u>licks</u> and **jumps,**
<u>licks</u> and **jumps,**
<u>licks</u> and **jumps.**
Pug the **pup**
<u>licks</u> and **jumps**
and <u>plays</u> in the **yard.**

Pug the **pup**
<u>pulls</u> and **tugs,**
<u>pulls</u> and **tugs,**
<u>pulls</u> and **tugs.**
Pug the **pup**
<u>pulls</u> and **tugs**
and <u>plays</u> in the <u>den.</u>

(Chant reproducible on page 49)

❶ Read *Pug the Pup* to the children. Point to each word, and read slowly as children follow top to bottom, left to right.

❷ Ask children to pantomime the words *licks, jumps, pulls,* and *tugs.*

❸ Read the chant again, and have children mime the words *licks, jumps, pulls,* and *tugs* as you read.

❹ Sing the chant to the tune of "London Bridge Is Falling Down." Have children listen and mime the words.

❺ Invite the children to join you as you sing *Pug the Pup* again.

❻ Distribute pre-made word cards for *licks, jumps, plays, yard, pulls, tugs,* and *den* to volunteers. Slowly read the chant with the children again. Ask the volunteers holding the appropriate cards to stand up on cue.

7 **Phonemic Awareness Strategy:** Tell children *Today we are listening for words that start with the same sound. If all three words start with the same sound, stand up. If all three words do not start with the same sound, cross your arms in front of your face to make a big X. Ready? Pug, pup, pulls. Tug, hug, rug. Tim, Tom, tug.*

8 **Letter/Word Awareness Strategy:**
Display the -ug phonogram using magnetic letters on a magnetic board. Add t to make tug, and have children read the word. Remove t and ask children what is needed to spell bug. Remove b and ask what is needed to spell jug, dug, mug, and hug. Mix up the letters on the magnetic board, and have children identify the letters b, d, g, h, j, m, t, and u.

9 **Blending Strategy:** Have children read the words Pug, hug, tug, jug, dug, bug, and mug. Have children extend their left arm as they say the beginning sound, extend their right arm as they say the phonogram, and pull both arms back as they read the word. (This is a review of the process used in previous books for phonogram blending practice.)

10 Display the chart or transparency of Pug the Pup. Point-track and sing the words as children join in.

When children have had sufficient practice with the rhythmic chant; recognize most new sight words; and seem confident with the suggested phonemic, letter/word awareness, and blending activities, they are ready to read Book 5.

1 Hold up Pug's Hugs. Ask open-ended questions such as What do you notice on the front cover of our book? and What do you think our story will be about? Identify the title, author, and illustrator.

2 **Metacognitive Coaching Strategy:**
Read the story as children listen. Pause on the word tugs. Think aloud how to decode the word. Say the beginning letter and its sound, and then recognize and read the phonogram -ug. Notice aloud that s is added to the familiar -ug. Blend aloud the beginning sound and phonogram. Then, say tug and add the s sound to the end. Read the word tugs. Go back and read the word in context, and then continue reading the book.

3 Distribute children's books. Read the story as children follow page by page. Call children's attention to the sight words come and then.

4 Slowly read the book aloud again, and have children read with you.

5 Have children read independently in a soft voice.

6 Have the children reread the story simultaneously with you. Observe each child's pace and fluency to assess progress.

Blending Phonograms
Distribute red, yellow, green, and one other color linking cubes and paper copies of the Pug the Pup reproducible (page 144) to the children in a reading group. Have each child link a yellow and a red cube to represent the phonogram -ug and place

the cubes on the reproducible. Invite children to read aloud /ug/. Have them add a green cube at the beginning of the chain to represent the letter *p*. Read it together as *Pug*. Tell the children *Say* Pug *without the /p/*. Ask children to take off the green cube (the /p/ sound) and say *ug*. Tell children *Say /m/ with* ug. Invite them to add a new color to the beginning and say *mug*. Continue this manipulation, addition, and deletion process to lead children to read by color-cube representation the words *Pug, bug, dug, hug, jug, lug, mug, rug,* and *tug*. This is practice with the phonemic-awareness skill of "onset-rime."

The Blending Tray Game

Place Alphabet Cards (pages 141–143) for *b, d, g, j, l, p, v,* and *y* in one small section of a TV-dinner tray. Place two *a* cards, two *o* cards, two *i* cards, and four *u* cards in the other small section. Select a consonant card and say its sound, holding the sound as you place the card in the tray's large section. Select a vowel card and, as you place it in the large section next to the consonant, blend the consonant's sound into the short vowel's sound. After you model this once, have children join in to finish the game together.

Pocket Chart Center

Place a copy of the rhythmic chant (*Pug the Pup*) in the pocket chart center. Invite one child to lead the song while other children follow along to practice reading the chant.

Overhead Projector Center

Use the Pug the Pup reproducible (page 144) to create a transparency. Place magnetic letters in a basket in the overhead projector center with the book *Pug's Hugs* or the rhythmic chant. Invite children to place letters on the Pup outline to create words from the story or chant and project them onto the wall.

Library Center

Place in the library center copies of the book *Pug's Hugs* and paper copies of the rhythmic chant. Place a tape recorder in the center. Invite children to tape-record themselves reading their new book and chant.

Pug the Pup

(to the tune of "London Bridge Is Falling Down")

Pug the pup
licks and jumps,
licks and jumps,
licks and jumps.
Pug the pup
licks and jumps
and plays in the yard.

Pug the pup
pulls and tugs,
pulls and tugs,
pulls and tugs.
Pug the pup
pulls and tugs
and plays in the den.

Dr. Maggie's Phonics Resource Guide © 1999 Creative Teaching Press

6 Jet It, Get It

FOCUS SKILLS z, x, short e

TRANSITION FROM BOOK 5 TO BOOK 6

Mushy Letters/Words

Fill resealable plastic freezer bags with two or three spoonfuls of fingerpaint (one bag per student). Press out the air as you seal the bags. Tape over the seal securely, and give each child a bag. Help children practice letters and sounds by calling out a letter sound or name and having them write the letter on their paint bag with their fingers. To have children practice word recognition, hold up a word card for them to recognize, read, and then copy on their paint bag. Continue the activity until children have practiced all previously learned and new letter/sound correspondences and most of the sight words from Books 1–5.

NEW WORDS

Focus-Skill Words

fi**x**

mi**x**

bo**x**

zap

zip

g**e**t

j**e**t

m**e**nd

s**e**nd

s**e**t

Sight Words

do

for

off

take

Story Words

buy

lunch

munch

pack

sack

snack

READY

Prior to this lesson, children should have been working with activities suggested for Book 5 to build phonemic and letter/sound awareness. These activities should have been extended to introduce *z, x,* and short *e* letter/sound correspondences.

Book 6 Rhythmic Chant
Bag It, Box It
(to the tune of "Ten Little Indians")

Bag it. **Box** it.
Zip it. **Zap** it.
Fix it. **Mix** it.
Mend it. **Send** it.
Set it. **Jet** it.
<u>Pack</u> it. <u>Sack</u> it.
<u>Munch</u> it <u>for</u> <u>lunch</u>.
Yum! Yum! Yum!

(Chant reproducible on page 54)

1 Read *Bag It, Box It* to children. Point to each word, and read slowly as the children follow top to bottom, left to right.

2 Read the chant again rhythmically, pointing to each word. Have children clap a steady beat as you read.

3 Sing the chant to the tune of "Ten Little Indians."

4 Sing the chant again with children participating.

5 Have children match word cards for *fix, mix, box, zap, zip, set, jet, munch, for,* and *lunch* to the words in the chant, line by line.

6 Place the word cards in a pocket chart. Have children read them aloud.

7 **Phonemic Awareness Strategy:** Place the following word pairs together in the pocket chart: *bag/box, fix/mix, set/jet,* and *zip/zap.* Ask children to tell where the word pairs sound the same—in the beginning or at the end.

8 **Letter/Word Awareness Strategy:** Display the -*et* phonogram using magnetic letters on a magnetic board. Add *b* to make *bet,* and have children read the word. Remove *b* and ask children what is needed to spell *get, jet, let, met, net, pet, set, vet, wet,* and *yet.* Mix up the letters on the magnetic board, and have children identify *b, e, g, j, l, m, n, p, s, t, v, w,* and *y.*

9 **Blending Strategy:** Write on a chalkboard or an overhead projector the words *bet, get, jet, let, met, net, pet, set, vet, wet,* and *yet* with the beginning letter in a different color for each word, but the phonogram the same color in all words. Have children extend their left arm as they say the beginning sound, extend their right arm as they say the phonogram, and pull both arms back in as they read the whole word.

10 Display the chart or transparency of *Bag It, Box It.* Point-track and sing the chant with the children to the tune of "Ten Little Indians."

READ

When children have had sufficient practice with the rhythmic chant; recognize most new sight words; and seem confident with the suggested phonemic, letter/word awareness, and blending activities, they are ready to read Book 6.

1 Hold up *Jet It, Get It*. Ask open-ended questions such as *What do you notice on the front cover of our book?* and *What do you think our story will be about?* Identify the title, author, and illustrator.

2 **Metacognitive Coaching Strategy:** Read the story as children listen. Pause on the words *bag* and *box*. Think aloud how both of those words have the same beginning sound but the rest of each word has different sounds. Pause on *zip* and *zap* to notice that both the beginning and the ending sounds are the same. Then continue reading the story.

3 Distribute children's books. Read aloud the story, one line at a time. Play a game called "Echo Maker." To play the game, hold your hands up to your mouth, distinctly read a line from the book, and have children respond by reading as an echo.

4 Read the book again as the children read aloud with you. Pause to call children's attention to the sight words *take, do, off,* and *for*.

5 Have children read independently in a soft voice. Move around the group, listen, and observe the children's progress with decoding words and recognizing sight words.

REVIEW

Blending Phonograms

Photocopy the Spinners reproducible (page 145). Divide the class into pairs, and give each pair a copy of the reproducible. Demonstrate how to create a pointer by placing the end of a paper clip on the center of each spinner and holding it in place with a pencil tip. Have children work in partners or groups, or call on volunteers in a whole-group setting. Have a child spin the beginning-letter spinner, say the letter sound, and record the letter on a piece of paper (or chalkboard, if working in a whole-group

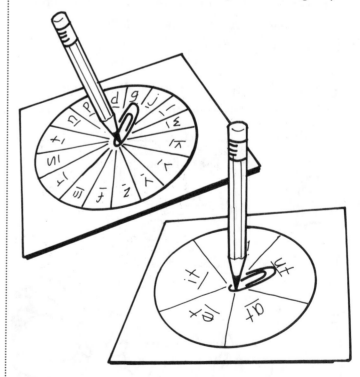

setting). Next, ask another child to spin the phonogram spinner, read the phonogram, and record the phonogram next to the beginning letter recorded previously. Then, have children read the word by blending the beginning sound and phonogram. Last, have children decide if the word is a real word or a "pretend" word (for example, *bat* versus *jat*).

The Blending Tray Game

Place Alphabet Cards (pages 141–143) for *b, j, l, m, n, p, s, t, v, w, y,* and *z* in one small section of a TV-dinner tray. Place two of each of the short *a, i, o,* and *u* vowel cards and six short *e* vowel cards in the other small section. Select a consonant card and say its sound, holding the sound as you place the card in the tray's large section. Select a vowel card and, as you place it in the large section next to the consonant, blend the consonant's sound into the short vowel's sound. After you model this once, have children join in to finish the game together.

Overhead Projector Center

Place the magnetic letters *b, e, j, l, m, n, p, s, t, v, w,* and *y* in a basket in the center. Invite children to manipulate the consonants with the short *e* vowel to create their own *-et* word family. Then, have them read the words.

Music Center

Place paper copies of the rhythmic chant *(Bag It, Box It)* in the music center along with rhythm instruments. When children are working at the center, have some quietly play a steady beat while others independently sing the chant to the tune of "Ten Little Indians."

Big Book Center

Have children copy the sentences from *Jet It, Get It* onto sentence strips at the big book center. Glue the strips onto large sheets of paper to create a big book. Have children illustrate each sentence, cut out their illustrations, and glue them into the big book. Invite children to read and reread their own version of *Jet It, Get It* to each other.

Bag It, Box It

(to the tune of "Ten Little Indians")

Bag it. Box it.

Zip it. Zap it.

Fix it. Mix it.

Mend it. Send it.

Set it. Jet it.

Pack it. Sack it.

Munch it for lunch.

Yum! Yum! Yum!

7 Click, Click

FOCUS SKILLS qu, ck

TRANSITION FROM BOOK 6 TO BOOK 7

Alphabet Time

Distribute an assortment of alphabet books and display an alphabet strip. Sing portions of "The Alphabet Song," such as "e, f, g" or "q, r, s" and point to the letters on the strip as you sing them. Have children find the letters in the books, point to them, and echo back that portion of the song. Then, challenge them to identify something that begins with each letter's sound.

NEW WORDS

Focus-Skill Words

qua**ck**

qui**ck**

ba**ck**pa**ck**

bu**ck**

cli**ck**

de**ck**

du**ck**s

ki**ck**

Ma**ck**

pa**ck**ed

Ri**ck**

ro**ck**s

sti**ck**

tu**ck**

Sight Word

we

Story Words

Gram

trip

Prior to this lesson, children should have been working with activities suggested for Book 6 to build phonemic and letter/sound awareness. These activities should have been extended to introduce *qu* and *ck* letter/sound correspondences.

Book 7 Rhythmic Chant
Rick and Mack
(to the tune of "Are You Sleeping?")

Rick and **Mack**
pack a **backpack**
for a <u>trip</u>, for a <u>trip</u>.
Quick, Rick, quick.
Quick, Mack, quick.
Click, click, click.
Click, click, click.

(Chant reproducible on page 59)

1 Read *Rick and Mack* to the children. Point to each word, and read slowly as children follow top to bottom, left to right.

2 Read the chant again rhythmically, pointing to each word.

3 Sing the chant to the tune of "Are You Sleeping?"

4 **Phonemic Awareness Strategy— Sound Detectives:** Have children investigate the words in the chant to discover the words that start with *qu*. Have them box the *qu* beginnings with their fingers or a wipe-off marker. Ask them *What does* qu *say?* (Work as a group, using a laminated chant chart, or give each student a copy of the chant reproducible.)

5 **Letter/Word Awareness Strategy— Word Detectives:** Distribute magnifying glasses to a few volunteers. Have these children investigate the words of the chant to discover how many words end with *ck*. Have them circle the *ck* endings and then count the words. Have other volunteers investigate the words to discover how many words start with *qu*. Have them count the words with *qu* beginnings and then count the words with *ck* endings. Read as a group all *qu* and *ck* words. Ask *What does* qu *say? What does* ck *say? What else makes the "hard* c*" sound?* Lead children to conclude that *c, k,* and *ck* all can say /k/.

6 **Blending Strategy:** Have children read the words *quick, click,* and *Rick.* Underline the *ick* in each word in one color and trace the *qu, cl,* and *R* in a different color. Lead children to blend the beginning sound(s) with the *-ick* phonogram to read the words.

7 Display the chant. As a group, read and sing the chant to the tune of "Are You Sleeping?" one more time to practice automaticity and word recognition.

 **READ**

When children have had sufficient practice with the rhythmic chant; recognize the new sight word; and seem confident with the suggested phonemic, letter/word awareness, and blending activities, they are ready to read Book 7.

❶ Hold up *Click, Click*. Ask open-ended questions such as *What do you notice on the front cover of our book?* and *What do you think our story will be about?* Identify the title, author, and illustrator.

❷ Ask children if they have ever gone on a trip and, if so, if they used a backpack to carry their belongings. Play a game called "Pack the Backpack" to prepare for reading the story. To prepare for the game, display a real backpack and the Click, Click Picture Cards (page 146). To play the game, distribute the picture cards to volunteers. Call each volunteer to the backpack by saying *Quick, quick, pack the _____,* inserting the name of one of the picture cards each time.

As they learn the game, invite children to say the *Quick, quick* part and you say the rest. When volunteers hear their picture being called, they quickly get up and pack it into the backpack. At the end of the game, say *Oh, no! We forgot the camera.* (Hold a real camera or the camera picture card, and pretend to take the children's picture.) *CLICK! CLICK!*

❸ Display the picture cards in a pocket chart. Add the backpack card. Have children read each card.

❹ Distribute children's copies of *Click, Click*. Have children read through each page and find the picture-card words in the text.

❺ Have children go back to the front cover and begin reading quietly.

❻ Reread the story at a slow pace and have the children read with you. Assess children's progress by noticing which children are decoding and recognizing sight words well and which children may be echoing their neighbor's reading.

Blending Phonograms

Create phonogram puzzles by duplicating another set of picture cards (page 146). Cut them apart between the beginning sounds and the -ck ending. Have children put these "puzzles" together, read the beginning sound, and blend the beginning sound to the phonogram.

Blending Sounds

Write each lowercase letter, except for *q* and *x,* on a round, white sticker. Make multiple sets of vowels. Have volunteers place a consonant sticker on one thumbnail and a vowel sticker on the other thumbnail. Sing *Where are thumbkins? Where are thumbkins?* Have the children hold up their thumbs and sing *Here we are. Here we are.* Then, sing to children *Can you read your thumbkins? Can you blend their sounds? Try it now. Try it now.* Have children hold their thumbs together and blend the consonant sound onto the short-vowel sound.

Pocket Chart Center

Place the Click, Click Picture Cards (page 146) and a backpack in the center. Have children read the cards and play "Pack the Backpack."

Music Center

Place paper copies of the rhythmic chant *(Rick and Mack)* in the center. Invite children to read and sing it to the tune of "Are You Sleeping?" You may also consider tape-recording the class singing the chant and including the tape at the center for sing-along practice.

Overhead Projector Center

Make a transparency of the rhythmic chant and place it in the center. Invite children to investigate the words in the chant and use overhead markers to identify categories of words such as -*ick* words, -*ack* words, *qu* words, or *ck* words.

Rick and Mack

(to the tune of "Are You Sleeping?")

Rick and Mack

pack a backpack

for a trip, for a trip.

Quick, Rick, quick.

Quick, Mack, quick.

Click, click, click.

Click, click, click.

8 The ABC Bags

FOCUS SKILLS double f, l, and s

TRANSITION FROM BOOK 7 TO BOOK 8

Scroll a Sound

Duplicate the Scroll-a-Sound reproducible (page 147), and give a copy to each child. Have children cut slits in the cat, the bed, the pig, the top, the van, and the mug. Invite children to cut out and scroll the short-vowel strip through the pictures. Have them practice blending and reading the words as they scroll.

NEW WORDS

Focus-Skill Words
Jeff
stiff
stuff
all
ball
calls
doll
hill
Nell
well
will
Will
yell
mess
Russ
Tess

Sight Words
asks
one
this
what

Story Words
egg
make
says

Prior to this lesson, children should have been working with activities suggested for Book 7 to build phonemic and letter/sound awareness and sight-word fluency. These activities should have been extended to introduce the double *f, l,* and *s* spellings at the end of one-syllable words (the "floss" rule).

Book 8 Rhythmic Chant
An ABC Song
(to the tune of "Twinkle, Twinkle, Little Star")

A B C D E F G
Jeff calls, "Make a **ball** for B."
H I J K L M N O P
Tess says, "Make one **doll** for D."
Q R S and T U V
This is **all.**
W X Y Z

(Chant reproducible on page 64)

1 Read *An ABC Song* to the children. Point to each word, and read slowly as children follow top to bottom, left to right.

2 Have children read the chant with you as you point to each word.

3 Sing the chant to the tune of "Twinkle, Twinkle, Little Star."

4 Sing the chant again with children participating.

5 Have children match double *f, l,* and *s* word cards (*Jeff, calls, ball, Tess, doll, all*) to words in the chant.

6 Place sight-word cards for *this* and *one* in a pocket chart. Have children read aloud these sight words and then match them to the chant.

7 **Phonemic Awareness Strategy:**
Ask children to listen as you say pairs of words such as *mess/Tess, stiff/stuff,* and *well/will.* Ask them to tell you where the words sound the same—at the beginning, in the middle, or at the end. Say the pairs of words again. This time ask them to tell you where the words sound different. This provides increasingly challenging practice with sound discrimination as children listen for beginning sounds, ending sounds, and finally, medial vowel sounds.

8 **Letter/Word Awareness Strategy:**
Tell children that you are going to write the words they just listened to so that they can see where the letters are the same and where they are different. Use magnetic letters to write the word pairs from Step 7, one above the other, on the chalkboard. Have children study the words and then describe where the words are the same and where they are different. Call children's attention to the double *l, s,* and *f* endings. Note that even though the letters are doubled, the sound remains the same.

9 **Blending Strategy:** Have children read aloud the words *hill, mess,* and *Jeff.* Write the beginning letter of each word on a bright green index card, the medial vowel on a bright yellow card, and the double-consonant ending on a bright pink card. Ask three sets of three volunteers to hold the cards for each word. Ask a child with a beginning letter to make the sound on his or her card, move close to the next child, and touch cards. As soon as the cards touch, have the middle child make his or her short-vowel sound and then touch the card to the ending sound card. Have the remaining children blend their sounds in the same way. This activity has children blend more than phonograms; they blend all three sounds.

10 Display the chart or transparency of *An ABC Song.* Point-track and sing the chant with the children to the tune of "Twinkle, Twinkle, Little Star."

When children have had sufficient practice with the rhythmic chant; recognize most new sight words; and seem confident with the suggested phonemic, letter/word awareness, and blending activities, they are ready to read Book 8.

1 Hold up *The ABC Bags.* Ask open-ended questions such as *What do you notice on the front cover of our book?* and *What do you think our story will be about?* Identify the title, author, and photographer.

2 **Metacognitive Coaching Strategy:** Read the story as children listen. Pause on the word *Russ.* Think aloud how to decode the word by saying the beginning letter and its sound, holding that sound and blending it to the medial vowel, and holding the vowel sound and blending it to the ending *s* sound. (This practice with successive blending is at a higher skill level than blending by phonogram alone.) Read the entire word. Go back and read the word in context, and then continue reading the book.

3 Distribute children's copies of *The ABC Bags.* Ask children to look through the book and locate the

words from the rhythmic chant's word cards (*Jeff, calls, ball, Tess, doll, all, this,* and *one*) in the book's text.

4 Have children slowly read the story simultaneously with you. Observe each child's level of ease with reading.

5 Have children reread independently in a soft voice. Move around the group, listen, and observe children's progress with decoding words and recognizing sight words.

Blending Phonograms

Since the *a* sound in *all* is neither the short *a* nor the long *a* sound, have children practice reading *all* as a phonogram. Create a transparency of the Word Family: -all reproducible (page 148) or enlarge it into poster size and laminate it. Have children read the word family represented at the top of the ball. On the following lines, add *b* to blend and read *ball, c* to blend and read *call, f* to blend and read *fall,* and so on for *hall, mall, tall, stall,* and *wall.* Ask children to reread the words. As they reread, have children extend their left arm as they say the beginning letter(s), extend their right arm as they say the phonogram, and pull both arms back in as they blend and read the entire word.

The Big Tray Blending Game

Obtain a TV-dinner tray with three small compartments at the top and one large section at the bottom. Place consonant letter cards in the left section, short-vowel cards in the middle section, and consonant and double *s, l,* and *f* cards in the right section. Demonstrate drawing one letter card from each section, isolating its sound, and placing it in the bottom section, one letter/sound at a time. (This models sound segmentation.) Then, make each letter's sound as you touch the cards together in the bottom part of the tray. Hold the sound as you touch the next letter and blend the first sound to the second. Then, blend the second sound to the third. This models successive blending, which is critical to children's fluent decoding and reading.

Music Center

Place a large copy of the rhythmic chant *(An ABC Song)* in the music center. Invite children to read, track the words, and sing the chant to the tune of "Twinkle, Twinkle, Little Star." You may wish to have other children play a xylophone or small bells as accompaniment.

Overhead Projector Center

Make a transparency copy of the Scroll-a-Sound reproducible (page 147) and place it in the center. Instead of pulling the strip through as done with the hard copy of the game, have children use transparent letter cards to manipulate the medial vowel changes. Challenge children to practice blending and reading the words. (Note: Invite them to use any of the vowel cards, even if they create nonsense words.)

Alphabet/Word Study Center

Place the letter cards and the big blending tray from the Review section in the center so children can practice blending with all consonants and medial vowels.

An ABC Song

(to the tune of "Twinkle, Twinkle, Little Star")

A B C D E F G

Jeff calls, "Make a ball for B."

H I J K L M N O P

Tess says, "Make one doll for D."

Q R S and T U V

This is all.

W X Y Z

9 Sing-Song Sid

TRANSITION FROM BOOK 8 TO BOOK 9

Word Puzzles

Reproduce the Word Puzzles on page 149. Have children cut them apart, manipulate them, and read each root word. Then, have children put the puzzle pieces back together and read the words with the *-ing* ending (*call-ing, pick-ing, stick-ing, yell-ing, say-ing, stay-ing, pack-ing, kick-ing, click-ing,* and *quack-ing*).

NEW WORDS

Focus-Skill Words
b**ing**
d**ing**
p**ing**
pl**ing**
s**ing**
s**ing**s
b**ong**
d**ong**
l**ong**
pl**ong**
p**ong**
s**ong**
b**ang**
d**ang**
p**ang**
pl**ang**

Sight Words
likes
sees
things
your

Story Words
buying
playing
ringing
tree

READY

Prior to this lesson, children should have been working with activities suggested for Book 8 to build phonemic awareness, letter/sound correspondence, and blending skills. These activities should have been extended to introduce the phonemes *-ing, -ang,* and *-ong.*

Book 9 Rhythmic Chant
Sing All Day Long
(to the tune of "Yankee Doodle")

Sing-Song Sid <u>likes</u> to **sing.**
He **sings** his **song** all day **long.**
He <u>sees</u> a <u>tree</u> in <u>your</u> yard
and makes up a **song.**

Sing, Sid, **sing** <u>your</u> **song,**
sing all day **long.**
Sing, Sid, **sing** <u>your</u> **song,**
sing <u>your</u> **song** all day **long.**

(Chant reproducible on page 69)

❶ Read *Sing All Day Long* to the children. Point to each word, and read slowly as children follow top to bottom, left to right.

❷ Read the chant again rhythmically, pointing to each word. Have children clap a steady beat as you read.

❸ Sing the chant to the tune of "Yankee Doodle."

❹ Sing the chant again with children participating.

❺ Place sight-word cards for *your, likes,* and *sees* in a pocket chart. Have children read aloud the sight words and match them to the chant text.

6 **Phonemic Awareness Strategy:**
Ask children to listen as you say the following word pairs: *sing/song, see/tree,* and *song/long.* Challenge them to determine where the words are the same and where they are different—in the beginning, the middle, or the end.

7 **Letter/Word Awareness Strategy:**
Create a chart with the *-ing* phonogram written six times in a column. Say an *-ing* word such as *bing, ding, ping, pling,* or *sing.* Each time you say a word, ask children which beginning letter(s) you will need to create the word. Write these letters on self-adhesive notes and attach them to the phonogram.

8 **Blending Strategy:** Continue the activity by having children blend the beginning sound(s) to the phonogram and read the words.

❾ Display the chart of *Sing All Day Long.* Point-track and sing with the children to the tune of "Yankee Doodle."

READ

When children have had sufficient practice with the rhythmic chant; recognize most new sight words; and seem confident with the suggested phonemic, letter/word awareness, and blending activities, they are ready to read Book 9.

1 Hold up *Sing-Song Sid*. Ask open-ended questions such as *What do you notice on the front cover of our book?* and *What do you think our story will be about?* Identify the title, author, and illustrator.

2 Ask children to demonstrate how a doorbell sounds. When they respond *ding-dong*, challenge them to make the sound begin with the letters *b, p, r, t,* and *s*. Tell the children that in this story, the main character, Sid, likes to play with the sounds of words. Each time he does, he makes up a song about things he sees.

3 As you read the story to the class, have children listen to the story to discover how many times Sid sees something and makes up a song about it.

4 Close the book. Encourage children to discuss what Sid sees in the story and what sounds he uses to describe what he sees.

5 **Metacognitive Coaching Strategy:**
Read the story again as children listen. Pause on the word *ringing*. Write the word on a chart. Look at the word, and think aloud how to decode the word. Say *I recognize the* -ing *part of this word. It says* /ing/. *I see* -ing *two times.* Cover up the ending *-ing* and look at the word *ring*. Say *The* r *says* /r/ *and* -ing *says* /ing/. *This word is* ring. *But I have another* -ing *here. What could this word be?* Ring *and* -ing *must say* ... *I know*—ringing! Go back to the book, read the word in context, and continue reading the book.

6 Distribute children's books. Write the words *playing, buying, things,* and *tree* on individual index cards. Hold up one card at a time, and have children find each word in the text.

7 Help the children extrapolate *playing* from their knowledge of the word *play*. For example, you might say *Take off the* pl, *and add* d *to say* day. *If* d-a-y *says* day, p-l-a-y *must say* play. Play *with* -ing *must say* playing. Help them read the other words from Step 6 in a similar manner.

8 Read the book again slowly, and have children read with you.

9 Have children read independently in a soft voice. Move around the group, listen, and observe children's progress with decoding words and recognizing sight words.

The Blending Tray Game

Refer to the original, three-section blending tray game (see Book 2's Review section, page 32). Place consonant cards *b, d, p, pl, r,* and *s* in the top left section. Place six *-ing* cards in the top right section. Draw a consonant card and an *-ing* card and place them in the bottom section of the tray. Blend the beginning sound(s) onto the *-ing* phonogram to read the word. After you model this once, have children continue the game until all cards have been blended.

Sticky Sounds

Write the following words in a column on a chart: *buy, play, ring, sing, pack, call, click, quack, jump,* and *snack*. Distribute to volunteers self-adhesive notes upon which the *-ing* ending has been written. Invite children to take turns selecting a word, reading the word, attaching an *-ing* note to it, and then reading the word with the *-ing* ending. When all children have played, ask the whole group to reread all the words in the column.

Music Center

Have children use rhythm band instruments to represent the sounds Sing-Song Sid makes in the story. Invite them to reread the book and, on each page that describes a sound, use an instrument to interpret the sound.

Song Box/Poetry Center

Place copies of the rhythmic chant *(Sing All Day Long)* in the center for children to read, point-track, and sing to the tune of "Yankee Doodle."

Library Center

Place in the library center copies of the book *Sing-Song Sid* for children to read and reread independently and with a partner.

Alphabet/Word Study Center

Place the consonant cards, the *-ing* phonogram cards, and the blending tray from the Review section in the center so children can practice blending *-ing* words. Also, place the "Sticky Sounds" chart and self-adhesive notes in the center so children can practice reading root words with *-ing* endings.

Sing All Day Long

(to the tune of "Yankee Doodle")

Sing-Song Sid likes to sing.
He sings his song all day long.
He sees a tree in your yard
and makes up a song.

Sing, Sid, sing your song,
sing all day long.
Sing, Sid, sing your song,
sing your song all day long.

10 Draw and Share

FOCUS SKILLS consonant digraphs: sh, ch, th

TRANSITION FROM
BOOK 9 TO BOOK 10

Flash and Read

Tape the following pairs of word cards around the room or write the word pairs on the chalkboard: *sip/ship, cat/chat, cap/chap, wit/with, hat/that, set/Seth, run/munch, top/shop,* and *hot/shot.* Turn out most of the lights. Shine a flashlight on one of the words without a digraph. Ask children to blend and read it. Take down each word or cross it off as you go. When all of the words without digraphs have been read by the children, give volunteers turns to flash the light and read the words with digraphs. At the end of the game, lead children to conclude what the letter "teams" *sh* and *ch* say and what two sounds letter team *th* can say.

NEW WORDS

Focus-Skill Words
di**sh**
fi**sh**
share
swi**sh**
wi**sh**
Chad
chat
chick
Be**th**
then
this

Sight Word
now

Story Words
draw
drum

READY

Prior to this lesson, children should have been working with activities suggested for Book 9 to build phonemic awareness, letter/sound correspondence, and blending skills. These activities should have been extended to introduce digraphs *sh*, *ch*, and *th*.

Book 10 Rhythmic Chant
Play Day
(to the tune of "Bingo")

Today is play day for **Chad** and **Beth,**
so they play "Draw and **Share."** OH!
A pig can jig
and a drum can hum.
A cat can scat
and a rat can **chat.**
A **dish** can **wish**
and a **chick** can click.
Now, that is "Draw and **Share."** OH!

(Chant reproducible on page 73)

1 Read *Play Day* to the children. Point to each word, and read slowly as children follow along top to bottom, left to right.

2 Pointing to each word, read the chant again with the children. Underline, circle, or highlight the new words *draw, now, drum,* and *share.* (Have children write on the chart only if you have laminated it first.)

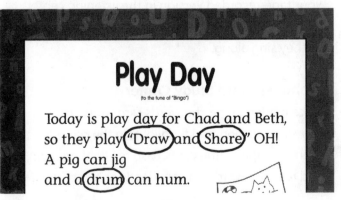

Play Day
(to the tune of "Bingo")

Today is play day for Chad and Beth,
so they play "Draw and Share" OH!
A pig can jig
and a drum can hum.

3 Sing the chant to the tune of "Bingo," and point only to each highlighted word.

4 Sing the chant again with children participating.

5 **Phonemic Awareness Strategy:** Ask children to listen and identify all rhyming word pairs in the chant (*pig/jig, drum/hum, cat/scat, rat/chat, dish/wish, chick/click*).

6 **Letter/Word Awareness Strategy:** Spell the rhyming words *pig* and *jig* on the overhead projector using transparent letter cards. Have children blend and read the words. Ask children to describe what they notice about these two words. Do the same for all other rhyming pairs from the chant. Encourage children to discuss what they notice about the letters in each pair of words and describe exactly how the words are similar and different.

7 **Blending Strategy:** Use the transparent letter cards to write these words: *cat, rat, chat, scat,* and *that.* Have children slowly blend the beginning sound(s) to the short vowel and hold the sound to blend it on to the ending sound. Then, have children read the words as quickly as they can.

8 Tape-record a final rendition of the class singing or reading the chant for use later in a listening center.

READ

When children have had sufficient practice with the rhythmic chant; recognize the new sight word; and seem confident with the suggested phonemic, letter/word awareness, and blending activities, they are ready to read Book 10.

1 Hold up *Draw and Share.* Ask open-ended questions such as *What do you notice on the front* *cover of our book?* and *What do you think our story will be about?* Identify the title, author, and illustrator.

 **Metacognitive Coaching Strategy:**
Distribute children's books. Read aloud the first line slowly as children follow. Stop and go back to notice that *today, play,* and *day* all end with the same sound. Model being a "Word Detective." Use your fingers to frame *day* in *today* and box in the entire word *day.* They are the same! Then box in *ay* in *today, play,* and *day.* Conclude aloud that *ay* must make the long *a* sound in some words. Act as if you are just thinking about this out loud, and mention that you will want to think some more about this at a later time (during Book 12, the long *a* book).

❸ Read aloud another page or two. Then ask children to take over the reading while you follow along. Have them read simultaneously but softly to the end of the story.

❹ Read the book again slowly, and have children read with you.

❺ Have children pair off and read to each other. Move around the group, listen, and observe children's progress with decoding words and recognizing the sight words.

 **Word Detective**
Display the words *Monday, Tuesday, Wednesday, Thursday, Friday, Saturday, Sunday,* and *today.* Have children investigate the words to find and highlight *day* in each word.

Blending Phonograms

Ask each child to draw a picture of a pig. Have children write *pig* and *jig* on their picture, one word above the other. Ask them to draw a drum and write *drum* and *hum* on that picture. Ask them to draw a cat and write *cat* and *scat* on that picture. After children have finished their drawings, ask them to read their words, covering the first letter(s), finding the phonogram, reading it, and then blending the beginning sound(s) onto the phonogram.

 **Big Book Center**
Write the text for *Draw and Share* on large sheets of paper bound together and place them in the center. Have children illustrate the text on construction paper, cut up their illustrations, and glue them onto the appropriate pages. Invite children to read and reread their own version of the story.

Listening Center
Place copies of the rhythmic chant *(Play Day)* with your tape-recorded version in the listening center. Invite children to play the tape and reread the chant as they sing along.

Alphabet/Word Study Center
Place masking tape, the words cards from the Transition section, and flashlights in the center so children can tape up the cards, flash the light on them, and read the words independently or to a partner.

Play Day

(to the tune of "Bingo")

Today is play day for Chad and Beth,
so they play "Draw and Share." OH!
A pig can jig
and a drum can hum.
A cat can scat
and a rat can chat.
A dish can wish
and a chick can click.
Now, that is "Draw and Share." OH!

11 Truck Tricks

FOCUS SKILLS consonant blends: tr, gr, dr, cr, fl

TRANSITION FROM BOOK 10 TO BOOK 11

Read-a-Ladder

Duplicate the Read-a-Ladder reproducible (page 150) and make seven transparency copies. Write *-at, -ed, -ig, -op, -um, -ick,* and *-ish,* each on the top rung of a separate transparency. With the children's help, write your way up the ladder by adding beginning sounds to each phonogram. Then, have children read each ladder to review and practice blending words and phonograms.

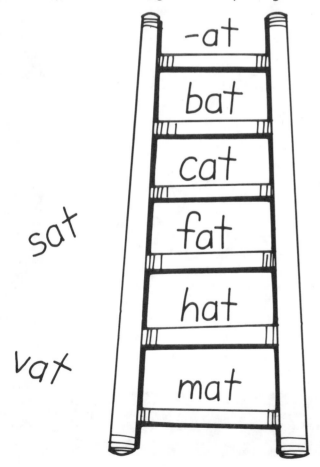

Prior to this lesson, children should have been working with activities suggested for Book 10 to build phonemic awareness, letter/sound correspondence, and blending skills. These activities should have been extended to introduce blends *tr, gr, dr, cr,* and *fl.*

Book 11 Rhythmic Chant
Vroom, Zoom, Boom!
(to the tune of "Jingle Bells")

Vroom, vroom, vroom.
Zoom, zoom, zoom.
Look out for monster **trucks.**
Off they go. They pick up speed so . . .
Look out, they **crash.** Oh, no!
Boom!

(Chant reproducible on page 78)

1 Read *Vroom, Zoom, Boom!* to the children. Point to each word, and read slowly as children follow top to bottom, left to right.

2 Read the chant again line by line. Have children reread each line after you, echo-chant style.

3 Sing the chant to the tune of "Jingle Bells."

4 Sing the chant again with children participating.

5 Place the sight-word cards *go, out,* and *look* in a pocket chart. Have children find the sight words in the rhythmic chant and highlight them. Reread the sight words as a group.

6 **Phonemic Awareness Strategy:**
Ask children to listen as you say pairs of words. Include some pairs in which the words are identical and others in which the words are similar;

for example, *trick/trick, trick/truck, tricks/trucks, crash/crush,* and *stop/stop.* If the words are the same, have children signal both thumbs up. If they are different, have them cross their arms to make a big X.

7 **Letter/Word Awareness Strategy:** Write *trick* and *tricks* at the top of a transparency, *truck* and *trucks* in the middle, and *crash* and *crush* at the bottom of the transparency. Place the transparency on the overhead projector, and turn off the lights. Project the words onto a surface low enough for children to reach the words. Have volunteers read the words in each row and touch the part of each word that is different.

8 **Blending Strategy:** Have children read a transparency or chart of the words *truck, trick, crash, crush,* and *stop.* (Write them as whole words and as words segmented into phonemes: *tr-u-ck, tr-i-ck, cr-a-sh, cr-u-sh,* and *st-o-p.*) Have children segment the words as indicated, blend the consonant blend onto the vowel, and then blend the vowel onto the final consonant to read the words.

truck	tr	u	ck
trick	tr	i	ck
crash	cr	a	sh
crush	cr	u	sh
stop	st	o	p

9 Display the chart or transparency of *Vroom, Zoom, Boom!* Point-track as children sing the words to the tune of "Jingle Bells."

READ

When children have had sufficient practice with the rhythmic chant; recognize most new sight words; and seem confident with the suggested phonemic, letter/word awareness, and blending activities, they are ready to read Book 11.

1 Hold up *Truck Tricks.* Ask open-ended questions such as *What do you notice on the front cover of our book?* and *What do you think our story will be about?* Identify the title, author, and illustrator.

2 Distribute the books. Ask children to find the dump truck in their books. Identify the pickup truck, the flatbed truck, and the monster trucks in the same way. Each time, have children repeat what kind of truck they are identifying.

3 Go back to the first page, and slowly read the story to the children as they follow word by word, page by page. Stop reading the story after the monster trucks crash. Invite children to talk about the ending. Ask what they think will happen next. Then read the end of the story. Ask if they were surprised.

4 Reread the story, and have children reread each page immediately after you do. This provides them with more practice with the story words.

5 Divide the class into groups of two or three, and have children read the book quietly but simultaneously. Watch carefully to determine how well they are reading the story words.

6 Have children reread the book with you. Notice and assess which children are able to read independently and which may need more practice.

REVIEW

Read-the-Word Speedway

Reproduce the Story Word Practice cards (page 151). Give each word card to a child, and have the children with the cards walk quickly in front of the class one at a time, pretending to race their trucks on a speedway. Invite the "spectators" to read the word on each truck card as it races by. (This activity builds fluency with story-word recognition.)

Blending Phonograms

Blend and read the words *buck, duck,* and *truck.* Have children use the familiar strategy of extending their left arm as they say the beginning sound(s), extending their right arm as they say the phonogram, and pulling both arms back in as they read the word.

REINFORCE

Library Center

Place in the center copies of the book *Truck Tricks* for children to read alone, with a partner, or to an older book buddy.

Music Center

Place copies of the rhythmic chant *(Vroom, Zoom, Boom!)* in the music center with jingle bells. Invite children to read the chant, play the bells, and sing the words to the tune of "Jingle Bells."

Overhead Projector Center

Place the Read-a-Ladder transparencies from the Transition section in the overhead projector center for children to "climb" and read independently.

Alphabet/Word Study Center

Place toy trucks in the center, and attach a piece of Velcro to the top or side of each truck. Make small word cards for the focus-skill words, sight words, and story words in *Truck Tricks.* Attach Velcro to the back of each card. Invite children to play "Read-the-Word Speedway" independently by having them attach a word to each truck and race it by a partner while the partner identifies the word. Make sure partners switch roles so both children have an opportunity to race cards and read words.

Vroom, Zoom, Boom!

(to the tune of "Jingle Bells")

Vroom, vroom, vroom.

Zoom, zoom, zoom.

Look out for monster trucks.

Off they go. They pick up speed so ...

Look out, they crash. Oh, no!

Boom!

 12 Dave and Jane's Band

FOCUS SKILLS long a: ay, a-e, ai

TRANSITION FROM BOOK 11 TO BOOK 12

Picture Words

Distribute to children word cards for *play, Dave, Jane, name, stage, rain, day, bay, hay,* and *pray* (each child should receive no more than one or two cards). Ask each child to draw a picture that illustrates the word cards he or she received. When the drawings are finished, mix up the word cards and the pictures, and have children read each word and match it to the appropriate picture.

NEW WORDS

Focus-Skill Words

aw**ay**

pl**ay**

pl**ay**s

st**ay**

tod**ay**

D**a**v**e**

Jan**e**

Jan**e**'s

m**a**k**e**

n**a**m**e**

sh**a**m**e**

st**a**g**e**

m**ai**n

r**ai**n

Sight Words

her

into

she

they

very

Story Words

guitar

loud

music

rain

Prior to this lesson, children should have been working with activities suggested for Book 11 to build phonemic awareness, letter/sound correspondence, and blending skills. These activities should have been extended to introduce the long *a* sound's letter pairings *(ai, a-e,* and *ay).*

Book 12 Rhythmic Chant
The Fat Cat Band
(to the tune of "Old MacDonald Had a Farm")

Dave and **Jane** have a fat cat band.
<u>They</u> **play** <u>very</u> <u>loud</u> **today.**
Jane plays <u>her</u> drums.
<u>She</u> **plays** so <u>loud</u>
the fat cats run **away.**

(Chant reproducible on page 83)

1 Read *The Fat Cat Band* to the children. Point to each word, and read slowly as children follow top to bottom, left to right.

2 Read the chant again rhythmically, pointing to each word. Have children clap a steady beat as you read.

3 Sing the chant to the tune of "Old MacDonald Had a Farm."

4 Sing the chant again with children participating.

5 Place in a pocket chart sight-word cards for *they, very, her,* and *she.* Have children read the sight words and then identify and highlight them in the chant.

6 Reread the chant, calling special attention to the sight words.

7 **Phonemic Awareness Strategy:**
Ask children to listen to pairs of words and describe the difference in each word of the pair. Include short-vowel/long-vowel pairs such as *Jan/Jane, man/main,* and *ran/rain.* Help children discover that a vowel can say its own name or it can make a short-vowel sound.

8 **Letter/Word Awareness Strategy:**
Write with transparent letter cards, cardstock letters, or magnetic letters the word pairs from Step 7. Have children examine them to discover how the words are different and what that difference does to the sound of the vowel. Lead them to articulate that when an *e* is at the end of the word it gives its voice to the vowel in the middle of the word and then remains silent. Explain that that is why *a* can say its name (make a long-vowel sound). Then, lead children to realize that when *a* and *i* come together they also make *a*'s long-vowel sound.

9 Display the chart or transparency of *The Fat Cat Band.* Have children identify long *a* words in the chant.

10 Review the chant again by singing it one more time as a student volunteer points to each word.

READ

When children have had sufficient practice with the rhythmic chant; recognize most new sight words; and seem confident with the suggested phonemic, letter/word awareness, and blending activities, they are ready to read Book 12.

1 Hold up *Dave and Jane's Band.* Ask open-ended questions such as *What do you notice on the front cover of our book?* and *What do you think our story will be about?* Identify the title, author, and illustrator.

2 Distribute children's books. Write the story words *loud, guitar,* and *music* on separate index cards. Have children look through the book to find these words.

3 Play a game called "You Go First!" Ask children to read the first page of the book to you. Then read the first page with them. Continue page by page for the first reading of the book.

4 Read the story to the children start to finish as they follow along and read aloud.

5 Have children read the story to you simultaneously in a soft voice. Listen and notice which children are reading with ease and which are struggling.

6 Have children pair off and read to each other as you assess their reading.

REVIEW

Working with Words

Reproduce the Long and Short *A* Word Cards (page 152). Have children cut the words apart and do a "word sort" according to vowel sounds. Have them place short *a* words in one group and long *a* words in another. For a more sophisticated activity, have children sort words according to the three ways to make the long *a* sound—*ay, a-e,* and *ai.*

The Blending Tray Game

Prepare beginning-sound cards *b, F, h, j, K, l, m, pl, r,* and *st* and place them in the top left section of a three-section TV-dinner tray. Place ten *ay* cards in the top right section. Invite children to take one card from each section and place it in the larger section. Have them blend and read the words *Fay, bay, Kay, ray, may, hay, jay, lay, play,* and *stay.*

Library Center

Place copies of the book *Dave and Jane's Band* in the library center along with erasable slates or small chalkboards and chalk. Invite children to reread the story and write all of the long *a* words on a slate or chalkboard. Challenge children to categorize the words according to the way they make the long *a* sound—*ay, a-e,* or *ai.*

Chart Center

Place a large copy of the rhythmic chant *(The Fat Cat Band)* in the chart center. Invite children to reread the chant independently and sing it to the tune of "Old MacDonald Had a Farm."

Alphabet/Word Study Center

Place the beginning-sound cards and the blending tray from the Review section in the center so children can practice blending words.

The Fat Cat Band

(to the tune of "Old MacDonald Had a Farm")

Dave and Jane have a fat cat band.
They play very loud today.
Jane plays her drums.
She plays so loud
the fat cats run away.

13 Pete's Street Beat

FOCUS SKILLS long e: ee, e-e, ea, ending e

TRANSITION FROM BOOK 12 TO BOOK 13

Slo-Mo Word and Go

Slowly pronounce the words *quack, stick, stiff, swish, chat, truck, share, beat, treat,* and *me* by segmenting their initial, medial, and final sounds. Stretch out the way you say them by talking in slow motion. Challenge children to blend each word before you go on to the next one.

NEW WORDS

Focus-Skill Words

f**ee**l

f**ee**t

m**ee**t

st**ee**l

str**ee**t

P**e**te's

b**ea**t

eat

n**ea**t

tr**ea**t

m**e**

Sight Word

sounds

Story Words

(none)

READY

Prior to this lesson, children should have been working with activities suggested for Book 12 to build phonemic awareness, letter/sound correspondence, and blending skills. These activities should have been extended to introduce the long *e*'s letter/sound correspondences *(ee, e-e, ea,* and ending *e)*.

Book 13 Rhythmic Chant
Street Beat with Pete

Street Beat.
Street Beat.
Pete's Street Beat
is a **treat.**

Street Beat.
Street Beat.
Street Beat <u>sounds</u>
are so **neat.**

(Chant reproducible on page 88)

1 Read *Street Beat with Pete* to the children. Point to each word, and read slowly as children follow top to bottom, left to right.

2 Read the chant again rhythmically, pointing to each word. Have children stand and stamp a steady beat with their feet as you read.

3 Have children sit and rhythmically read the chant with you as you point to the words.

4 Have children match word cards for *street, beat, treat, Pete,* and *neat* to words in the chant.

5 Place the word cards from Step 4 in a pocket chart. Have children read the words again. Add the word card *sounds* to the pocket chart, and

help children read the *s, n, d,* and ending *s.* Tell them *ou* says /ow/ in this word. Read the word *sounds,* and then have children read it.

6 **Phonemic Awareness Strategy:** Ask children to listen as you say slowly, emphasizing the medial sound, *street, beat, treat, Pete,* and *neat.* Ask the children what they notice about these words. Have them describe their observations about the sounds.

7 **Letter/Word Awareness Strategy:** Write the words *street, beat, treat, neat,* and *Pete* with magnetic letters or transparent letter cards on an overhead projector. Point to each word and say it slowly. Have children repeat it. Categorize the words based on the way the long *e* sound is spelled. Put *street* on the left side of the overhead; *beat, neat,* and *treat* in the middle; and *Pete* on the right. Have children play "Word Detective" to analyze and describe the letters that make the long *e* sound. Help children articulate that, just as with long *a,* several letter combinations can make the long *e* sound—*ee, ea,* and *e* with a silent *e* on the end. Also, *e* by itself (as in *me, she,* and *he)* can make the long *e* sound. Spell *me, he,* and *she* with transparency letter cards, and project them as you describe this other way to make the long *e* sound.

8 **Blending Strategy:** Have children read the words *beat, neat,* and *treat.* Have children extend their left arm as they say the beginning sound(s), extend their right arm as they say the phonogram *(-eat),* and pull both arms back as they read the word.

9 Display the chart of *Street Beat with Pete.* Point-track as children read rhythmically, but this time have two or three volunteers play accompaniment on drums or other rhythm instruments. Tape-record this last rendition for later use in a listening center.

When children have had sufficient practice with the rhythmic chant; recognize the new sight word; and seem confident with the suggested phonemic, letter/word awareness, and blending activities, they are ready to read Book 13.

1 Hold up *Pete's Street Beat.* Ask open-ended questions such as *What do you notice on the front cover of our book?* and *What do you think our story will be about?* Identify the title, author, and illustrator.

2 Distribute children's books. Read the book to the children slowly, one page at a time. Pat a table or drum on each word. This will help children internalize the rhythm of the language in this book. Have children echo-read each page back to you as you continue tapping the beat.

3 **Metacognitive Coaching Strategy:** Reread the story to the children. When you get to pages 6–8, pause to note that these words describe sounds. Explain to children that sometimes words sound like the things they are describing; for

example, *ding-dong, rat-a-tat,* and *ring-a-jing.* Ask children *In what other book did we have words like this? (Sing-Song Sid.)* Continue reading the story while children follow and track the words.

4 Reread the book but tell children that this time they will read the pages with words that describe sounds as you listen.

5 Have children read independently in a soft voice. Move around the group, listen, and observe children's progress.

Blending Sounds
Write the words *street, beat, treat, feet, meet,* and *neat* on separate index cards or sheets of construction paper (each word on a different color card or paper). In front of the children, say each word slowly and create three-piece puzzles by cutting off the beginning and ending sounds. Have volunteers take each puzzle, manipulate it, and blend the sounds to read the word.

Word Investigation Time

Make a copy of the My Word Sort reproducible (page 153) for each child. Fill in the title line to say *Long* e *Word Sort,* and fill in the four columns with *ee, ea, e-e,* and *ending e.* Read and explain these columns to the children. Distribute copies of the book *Pete's Street Beat.* Have children reread the book, write all long *e* words on small self-adhesive notes, and then sort the words onto their paper.

Overhead Projector Center

Place in the center word cards used in the Ready section, Step 4; a basket of transparency letter cards or magnetic letters; and a copy of the rhythmic chant *(Street Beat with Pete).* Invite children to read the chant, locate the words on the word cards, reproduce them using letters on the overhead, project them onto the wall, and read them.

Alphabet/Word Study Center

Place in the center the word puzzles and copies of the reproducible from the Review section and a few copies of the book. Invite children to revisit the blending and word-identification strategies learned during the Ready section.

Listening Center

Place in the listening center copies of the book *Pete's Street Beat* and the cassette tape made during an earlier reading for children to follow along and reread.

Music Center

Place drums and rhythm band instruments in the center for children to create their own "street beat" sounds as they reread *Pete's Street Beat.*

Street Beat with Pete

Street Beat.

Street Beat.

Pete's Street Beat

is a treat.

Street Beat.

Street Beat.

Street Beat sounds

are so neat.

14 Twice as Nice

FOCUS SKILLS long i: i-e

TRANSITION FROM
BOOK 13 TO BOOK 14

Word Wheels

Prepare for each child a set of Alphabet Cards (pages 141–143) and a "word wheel." Make each word wheel by holding the tops of two butter-tub lids together and poking a metal fastener through the center of both lids. (You may want to ask children to bring in two lids each to ease your preparation.) Have each child cut apart the cards and color the vowel cards red. Display the chants from Books 13 and 14 as well as any word cards from previous books children need to review. Call out or point to a word card or a word in the chant, and challenge children to spell out the word by inserting letter cards into their word wheel between the two lids. On your signal, have children hold up their words so you can assess their accuracy. Repeat this activity for several words.

NEW WORDS

Focus-Skill Words

bike

mice

Miles

nice

Pine

Stine

twice

wise

Sight Words

are

good

my

Story Words

Mr.

Mrs.

orange

teacher

yellow

Prior to this lesson, children should have been working with activities suggested for Book 13 to build phonemic awareness, letter/sound correspondence, and blending skills. These activities should have been extended to introduce the long *i*'s letter/sound correspondence *(i-e)*.

Book 14 Rhythmic Chant
Can't Be Beat!

Twice as <u>good</u>,
twice as sweet,
twice as **nice,**
twice as neat.

Red, <u>orange</u>, <u>yellow</u>,
blue, and peach.
<u>My</u> <u>teachers</u> <u>are</u> **wise**
and can't be beat!

(Chant reproducible on page 93)

1 Read *Can't Be Beat!* to the children. Point to each word of the chant, and read slowly as children follow top to bottom, left to right.

2 Underline the words *good, sweet, nice, neat, yellow, peach, wise,* and *beat.* Read these words to the children and have them repeat each one.

3 Read the chant again rhythmically, pointing to each word. Stop on each underlined word. Have children provide a cloze to each sentence by having them read the underlined word.

4 Read the chant again in unison.

5 **Phonemic Awareness Strategy:**
Ask children to close their eyes and listen to the chant for words that rhyme. Then, practice generating rhyming words. Say a word from the chant and have children supply a rhyme for it.

6 **Letter/Word Awareness Strategy:**
Display a color-word chart. Have children locate in the chant the words *red, orange, yellow, blue,* and *peach*. Ask them to find these words in the color-word chart.

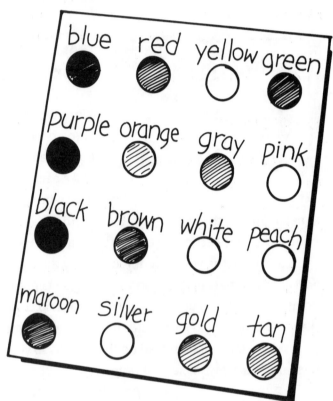

7 **Blending Strategy:** Have children blend *green, tree, nice, mice, mine, pine, wise,* and *neat.* Have children extend their left arm as they say the beginning sound(s), extend their right arm as they say the phonogram, and pull both arms back as they read the word.

8 Display the chart or transparency of *Can't Be Beat!* Point-track and read rhythmically with children in unison.

READ

When children have had sufficient practice with the rhythmic chant; recognize most new sight words; and seem confident with the suggested phonemic, letter/word awareness, and blending activities, they are ready to read Book 14.

1 Hold up *Twice as Nice*. Ask open-ended questions such as *What do you notice on the front cover of our book?* and *What do you think our story will be about?* Identify the title, author, and illustrator.

2 Distribute children's books.

3 **Metacognitive Coaching Strategy:** Ask children to read the book silently (or as quietly as possible). Remind them to pause on any word they do not recognize and look at every letter in the word. Ask them to think about what they know about the sounds those letters make. Have them try to find a familiar word family "hiding" in the word. Ask them to decide if it is a color word or sight word they have seen before.

4 Reread the story with the children in unison.

5 Have children read independently in a soft voice. Move around the group, listen, and observe children's progress with decoding words and recognizing sight words.

REVIEW

Blending Phonograms
Write the following words in a column on the chalkboard or on a chart: *ice, dice, lice, mice, nice, price, rice, slice, twice,* and *vice*. Write the *-ice* phonogram in one color, but change the color of each word's beginning letter(s). Have children practice reading the words, blending the beginning sound(s) onto the phonogram.

Word Wise
Ask children to look at a word you write on the overhead and "take a picture of it" in their mind. Silently count to five. Turn off the overhead, and ask children to write the word on scratch paper. Turn the overhead back on, and let children check their word. Consider using words such as *mice, nice, rice,* and *my*. Ask the children *What did you notice about the* i *in the words* mice, nice, *and* rice? *In each word,* e *was at the end. Silent* e *makes the* i *long and then stays quiet. What did you notice about the* y *sound in* my? Lead children to conclude that sometimes a *y* at the end of a word can sound like long *i* just like the *i* in a word that ends with *e* can make the long *i* sound.

Overhead Projector Center

Place a basket of transparent letter cards or magnetic letters in the overhead projector center so children can create long *i* words that appear in the story and project them onto the wall for other children to read.

Poetry Box Center

Place copies of the rhythmic chant (*Can't Be Beat!*) in the poetry box center. Invite children to reread the text to discover rhyming words, long *i* words, long *e* words, and familiar sight words. Make self-adhesive notes, rubber bands, or markers available for children to frame or highlight the words as they locate them.

Library Center

Place an assortment of alphabet books in the library center. Invite children to locate words that begin with each short vowel sound and then find words that begin with the long *a*, *e*, and *i* sounds. Invite them to record their findings on small notepads or self-adhesive notes.

Alphabet/Word Study Center

Place color-word charts and books in the center so children can read and identify the color words *green*, *gray*, *red*, *orange*, *yellow*, *blue*, and *peach*. Invite them to then draw or water-color a rainbow of these colors. When the illustrations are dry, have children appropriately label each color of the rainbow.

Can't Be Beat!

Twice as good,
twice as sweet,
twice as nice,
twice as neat.

Red, orange, yellow,
blue, and peach.
My teachers are wise
and can't be beat!

15 The Little Green Man Visits Pine Cone Cove

FOCUS SKILLS long o: o-e, oa, ow, ending o; -old

TRANSITION FROM BOOK 14 TO BOOK 15

Blast Off to Good Reading

Sketch on poster board a large spaceship with portholes. Select words your children need to review from previous books, write these words on self-adhesive notes, and attach each word to a porthole. Have children count down the words they can read. Tell them that to "blast off" they have to work together to read all of the words. When they have read these words, pretend to have "liftoff" by lifting the poster board over your head and pretending the ship is flying. Then, land the ship, and replace the words with long *o* words. See if children can use their knowledge about long *a, e,* and *i* words to decode long *o* words that use the silent *e* pattern, such as *cone, cove, doze, hole, nose, pole, robe, rope,* and *tote.*

NEW WORDS

Focus-Skill Words
c**o**n**e**
c**o**v**e**
d**o**z**e**
h**o**l**e**
n**o**s**e**
p**o**k**e**s
p**o**l**e**
r**o**b**e**
r**o**p**e**
t**o**t**e**
b**oa**t
c**oa**t
bl**ow**s
l**ow**
sl**ow**
t**ow**s
J**o** J**o**
s**o**
c**old**
f**old**s
h**old**s

Sight Words
from
head
little

Story Words
anymore
starts
visits

READY

Prior to this lesson, children should have been working with activities suggested for Book 14 to build phonemic awareness, letter/sound correspondence, and blending skills. These activities should have been extended to introduce the long *o*'s letter/sound correspondence *(o-e, oa, ow,* ending *o)* and the phonogram *-old.*

Book 15 Rhythmic Chant
Low in the Cove
(to the tune of "This Old Man")

Low in the **cove**
<u>from</u> up in space,
the <u>little</u> green man says,
"What a nice place!"
With **Jo Jo** to **tow**
the <u>little</u> orange ship,
the <u>little</u> green man
<u>starts</u> off on a trip.

(Chant reproducible on page 98)

1 Read *Low in the Cove* to the children. Point to each word, and read slowly as children follow top to bottom, left to right.

2 Highlight the words *low, cove, Jo Jo,* and *tow.*

3 Ask children to listen for the sounds made in each of these words as you read and point to each word in the chant again.

4 Sing the chant to the tune of "This Old Man." Then, highlight in a different color the words *from, little,* and *starts* and read them to the children.

5 Sing again, and have children sing with you as you point to each word.

6 **Phonemic Awareness Strategy:** Ask children to listen again to the words you highlighted in Step 2 and tell you what they notice about the vowel sound in each. Guide them to note the long *o* sound in each word.

7 **Letter/Word Awareness Strategy:** Write the words *low, cove, Jo Jo,* and *tow* on separate index cards. Have children match the cards to the chant. Read each word as it is matched. Conclude that the long *o* sound can be made by *ow, o* with a silent *e,* and *o* by itself at the end of a word.

8 Display the chart or transparency of *Low in the Cove.* Point-track and have children read and sing the song in unison.

READ

When children have had sufficient practice with the rhythmic chant; recognize most new sight words; and seem confident with the suggested phonemic, letter/word awareness, and blending activities, they are ready to read Book 15.

1 Hold up *The Little Green Man Visits Pine Cone Cove.* Ask open-ended questions such as *What do you notice on the front cover of our book?* and *What do you think our story will be about?* Identify the title, author, and illustrator.

2 Read the story page by page as children listen.

3 Distribute children's books. Read the story page by page with children following along. After each page, have the children read the page back to you in unison.

4 **Metacognitive Coaching Strategy:**
Have children look through the first pages to find a word spelled *c-o-n-e.* Ask them to read the word and explain how they know how the word is pronounced. (Children should be able to verbalize recognition of the silent *e* pattern.) Follow the same procedure to locate, spell, and ask for verbalization of the decoding strategy used for the words *boat, low,* and *no.*

5 Have children read independently in a soft voice. Move around the group, listen, and observe children's progress with decoding words and recognizing sight words.

6 Have children reread the story simultaneously with you. Observe each child's pace and fluency to assess progress.

Blending Phonograms

Have children practice blending to read the following words: *cold, fold,* and *hold; boat, coat,* and *goat;* and *low, tow, blow,* and *slow.* Write the phonogram in each set of words on a separate sentence strip. Place a beginning sound written on a self-adhesive note in front of the phonogram, and have children practice changing the beginning sound. Attach one note on top of the other until all words have been formed. Staple the notes in place to create a "lift-the-flap" phonogram game.

Blending Sounds

Help children practice blending a beginning consonant onto the long *o* sound by having them connect different-color beginning-sound linking cubes to a red linking cube labeled *o.* Have students attach cubes labeled *g, h, J, n,* and *s* to create, blend, and read the words *go, ho, Jo, no,* and *so.*

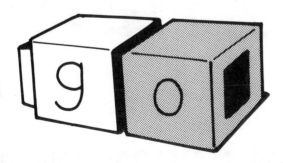

Art Center

Have children draw or paint a scene of the little green man and his orange ship in Pine Cone Cove. Invite children to use their knowledge of spelling-sound relationships to label objects in the picture. For example, children might label the little green man, the little orange ship, Pine Cone Cove, Jo Jo, a hole, a pole, a rope, or a coat.

Music Center

Place rhythm instruments and copies of the rhythmic chant *(Low in the Cove)* in the music center. Invite children to play accompaniment as they read and sing the chant to the tune of "This Old Man."

Library Center

Place in the library center copies of the book *The Little Green Man Visits Pine Cone Cove* and the copy of the rhythmic chant on which you highlighted the words *low, cove, Jo Jo,* and *tow* (see Ready section, Step 2). Invite children to read the chant to find highlighted words and then read the book to see if the words appear in the book text as well as in the chant text.

Low in the Cove

(to the tune of "This Old Man")

Low in the cove
from up in space,
the little green man says,
"What a nice place!"
With Jo Jo to tow
the little orange ship,
the little green man
starts off on a trip.

16 Mr. Noisy at the Dude Ranch

TRANSITION FROM BOOK 15 TO BOOK 16

Way Out West

Seat a small group of children in a circle. Talk about going "way out west" where cowboys and cowgirls live on a ranch, rope cattle, sleep out under the stars, and so on. (This game helps you to determine children's existing knowledge about the old west and helps you to build knowledge in preparation for the new book.) Start the game by saying *Way out west, I will see boots.* Continue the game around the circle by having children name items they will see way out west (for example, a ranch, cows, a mule, a rope, or a horse). Have each child name all the items previously mentioned and add a new one to the story. After everyone in the group has had a turn, write each item down on a small cow- or horse-shaped cutout and tape it into a paper fence "corral." Be sure to add the words *dude, mule, ranch, rope, sunup,* and *sunset* to the corral if they were not mentioned. Read the words in the corral and have children reread them in unison. Encourage children to use their existing knowledge about silent *e* to read *dude, mule,* and *rope.* Help children find little words they recognize within the words *sunup* and *sunset.*

NEW WORDS

Focus-Skill Words

cute	tune
dude	use
Duke	join
huge	noise
Jules	Noisy
June	oil
Luke	boy
Luke's	Roy
mule	toy

Sight Word

when

Story Words

boots
howdy
Lucky
ranch
roped
Rudy
sunset
sunup
waved
yee-hah
yelled

READY

Prior to this lesson, children should have been working with activities suggested for Book 15 to build phonemic awareness, letter/sound correspondence, and blending skills. These activities should have been extended to introduce the long *u*'s letter/sound correspondence *(u-e)* and the /oi/ sound's letter/sound correspondences *(oi, oy)*.

Book 16 Rhythmic Chant
Dude Ranch Fun
(to the tune of "Bingo")

Mr. **Noisy** went to the **dude** ranch.
He had lots of fun. OH!
He met **Jules** and **June.**
He rode Rudy the **mule.**
He sang with **Duke** and **Roy,**
and he had lots of fun. OH!

(Chant reproducible on page 103)

1 Read *Dude Ranch Fun* to the children. Point to each word, and read slowly as children follow top to bottom, left to right.

2 Read the chant again rhythmically, pointing to each word. Have children clap a steady beat as you read.

3 Sing the chant to the tune of "Bingo." Highlight the words *dude, Jules, June, Rudy, mule,* and *Duke.* Pronounce them distinctly, emphasizing the *u* sound in each.

4 Sing the chant again with children participating.

5 **Phonemic Awareness Strategy:**
Ask children to listen as you say the following pairs of words: *Jules/mules, Jules/June, Duke/duck,* and

Rudy/Judy. Have them describe where the sounds are alike and where the sounds are different in the word pairs.

6 **Letter/Word Awareness Strategy:** Write the words *Jules* and *mules* on separate index cards. Hold one card directly above the other. Ask children what they notice about the letters in the words. Do the same for *June* and *tune* and *Rudy* and *Judy.*

7 **Blending Strategy:** Write *rope* and *wave* on separate index cards. Call children's attention to the silent *e* in each word. Ask them what the *e* does to the vowel sound. Help children blend /r/ /oa/ /p/ to read *rope* and /w/ /ay/ /v/ to read *wave.* Next, write a *d* on two self-adhesive notes and stick them on the end of *rope* and *wave.* Show children how to blend the ending sound onto *rope* and *wave* to read *roped* and *waved.* Call their attention to the sound the *d* makes in each word.

8 Display the chart or transparency of *Dude Ranch Fun.* Point-track as children sing the chant to the tune of "Bingo."

READ

When children have had sufficient practice with the rhythmic chant; recognize the new sight word and seem confident with the suggested phonemic, letter/word awareness, and blending activities, they are ready to read Book 16.

1 Hold up *Mr. Noisy at the Dude Ranch.* Ask open-ended questions such as *What do you notice on the front cover of our book?* and *What do you think our story will be about?* Identify the title, author, and illustrator.

2 Distribute children's books. Ask the children to read the story silently (or as quietly as possible) as best they can.

3 **Metacognitive Coaching Strategy—Reading for Information:** Ask children to reread the first two pages to find the part of the story where Mr. Noisy has a problem. Then, ask them to read until they find the part that tells who helped Mr. Noisy with his problem, the part that tells where Mr. Noisy went, the part that names all the new people Mr. Noisy met, the part that tells what he got from his new friends, the part that lists the things Mr. Noisy did at the dude ranch, and the part that tells what happened when Mr. Noisy's problem was fixed. Ask children *Based on all you read so far, what do you think a dude ranch is?*

4 Slowly reread the book in unison with the children.

5 Have children read independently in a soft voice. Move around the group, listen, and observe children's progress with decoding words and recognizing sight words.

REVIEW

Word Work

Type all focus-skill words on a sheet of paper, and laminate the paper. Cut the words apart and place them on a My Word Sort reproducible (page 153). Have children play "Word Detectives" (see Book 7's Ready section, page 56) to carefully study the letters in each word and sort words according to long *u* words with silent *e*, *oi* words, and *oy* words.

REINFORCE

Writing Center

Have children use pictures and words to create their own stories about going to a dude ranch. Encourage them to use words from the story to practice writing and reading long *u* words. Make available copies of the rhythmic chant *(Dude Ranch Fun)* and the book *Mr. Noisy at the Dude Ranch*. Children can refer to these for the spelling of words they want to use in their stories.

Magnetic/Flannel Board Center

Place in the center the character cutouts and name cards from the Mr. Noisy and Friends reproducible (page 154). Attach a flannel or magnetic strip to the back of each cutout or card. Invite children to match name cards to characters and create their own scenarios at the dude ranch.

Music Center

Play country/western music quietly in the background in the music center as children reread *Mr. Noisy at the Dude Ranch*.

Alphabet/Word Study Center

Place in the center copies of the My Word Sort reproducible (page 153) and the focus-skill-word cards used in the Word Work activity of the Review section so children can practice sorting words into long *u* words, *oi* words, and *oy* words.

Dude Ranch Fun

(to the tune of "Bingo")

Mr. Noisy went to the dude ranch.
He had lots of fun. OH!
He met Jules and June.
He rode Rudy the mule.
He sang with Duke and Roy,
and he had lots of fun. OH!

17 Sad Sam and Blue Sue

FOCUS SKILLS oo, ue

TRANSITION FROM BOOK 16 TO BOOK 17

Beanbag Word Relay

Write each of the following words on a separate index card with Velcro attached to the back: *truck, grass, play, name, rain, meet, beat, me, bike, mice, twice, cone, rope, boat, slow, cold, dude, mule, oil, boy, toy, ranch,* and *boots.* Attach a Velcro strip to two beanbags. Divide the class into two relay teams, and have each team stand in a line. Divide the word cards into two equal piles and place them facedown. At your signal, the first person in each line picks up a card using the Velcro on the beanbag, reads the word aloud, pulls the word card off the beanbag, puts the beanbag and word card down, and goes to the back of the line. The next person from each team picks up a new card, reads it, pulls off the word card, puts the beanbag and card down, and goes to the back of the line. This continues until the first players are at the front of the lines again. When the game is over, find the word *boots.* Have children read it. Block off the letters to isolate the *oo.* Say the /oo/ sound. Reveal the word again, and read *boots.*

NEW WORDS

Focus-Skill Words

too

blue

Sue

Sue's

Sight Words

(none)

Story Words

friend

outside

sorry

READY

Prior to this lesson, children should have been working with activities suggested for Book 16 to build phonemic awareness, letter/sound correspondence, and blending skills. These activities should have been extended to introduce *oo* and *ue* letter/sound correspondences.

Book 17 Rhythmic Chant
So Sad, So Blue

I feel sad.
I feel **blue, too.**
You miss your <u>friend</u>?
I am <u>sorry</u> for you.
Blue, blue,
I feel **blue.**
Blue, too?
I am <u>sorry</u> for you.

(Chant reproducible on page 108)

❶ Read *So Sad, So Blue* to the children. Point to each word, and read slowly as children follow top to bottom, left to right.

❷ Read the chant again as children read with you.

❸ Divide the class into two groups, and read the chant call-and-response style. Have the groups alternate reading each line.

4 **Phonemic Awareness Strategy:**
Ask children to listen as you say the words *blue, too,* and *you.* Ask children what they notice about the endings of these words.

5 **Letter/Word Awareness Strategy—**
Reading by Analogy: Write the words *boots, too,* and *blue* on separate index cards. Display the cards. Ask children to look at the word *too,* think about the word *boots,* and try to read the word. Next, hold up the word *blue.* Cover the *bl* to reveal the *ue.* Help children determine that the /oo/ sound can be made by *oo* and by *ue.* Read *boots, too,* and *blue* one more time.

❻ Display the chant *So Sad, So Blue.* Point-track as children read in unison. Tape-record this last reading for use in a listening center.

READ When children have had sufficient practice with the rhythmic chant and seem confident with the suggested phonemic, letter/word awareness, and blending activities, they are ready to read Book 17.

1 Hold up *Sad Sam and Blue Sue.* Ask open-ended questions such as *What do you notice on the front cover of our book?* and *What do you think our story will be about?* Identify the title, author, and illustrator.

2 Distribute children's books. Ask children to read with you in a soft voice as you read the story aloud.

3 Have children reread the story silently (or as quietly as possible). Observe which children seem to be reading well and which are having difficulty.

4 Reread the story page by page, echo-chant style. (Read one page and have the children reread it as you observe and listen.)

5 **Metacognitive Coaching Strategy:**
Write the word *outside* on an index card and hold it up. Ask children to find the page with this word on it. Ask children *What could we do to read this big word?* Model for children how to frame off the parts of the word to reveal that the large word is made of two small words that are easier to read. Together, read the word *outside.*

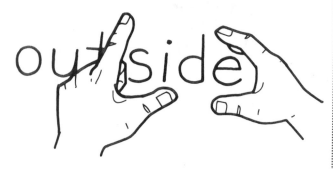

6 Have children read independently in a soft voice. Move around the group, listen, and observe children's progress with decoding words and recognizing sight words.

REVIEW **Stretch the Word**
Write each of the following words on a separate elastic strip: *cat, glad, mule, bike,* and *boy.* Leave space between each letter, except for the *oy* in *boy.* Hold the *cat* strip in front of the children, stretch out the strip, and have children pronounce each sound (/c/ /a/ /t/). Then, slowly release the strip, and ask them to blend the word *cat.* Repeat this process for the remaining words, and point out the silent *e* in *mule* and *bike.*

REINFORCE

Chart Center

Place the rhythmic chant *(So Sad, So Blue)* in the chart center. Invite children to work in pairs to practice reading the chant call-and-response style.

Overhead Projector Center

Place a transparency of the rhythmic chant in the center. Invite children to use overhead pens to highlight all words with the /oo/ sound made by *oo* and *ue*. Also, invite them to box off story words, underline small words within big words, and practice other skills presented during this section.

Listening Center

Place paper copies of the rhythmic chant and your tape-recorded version of the chant in the center for children to listen to and read along with.

Alphabet/Word Study Center

Place an assortment of letter cards, magnetic letters, and word cards in the center for children to manipulate to practice blending sounds and making words.

So Sad, So Blue

I feel sad.

I feel blue, too.

You miss your friend?

I am sorry for you.

Blue, blue,

I feel blue.

Blue, too?

I am sorry for you.

18 Out to Gumball Pond

TRANSITION FROM BOOK 17 TO BOOK 18

Cross the River

Cut out some paper stepping stones and write on them sight words and story words children still need to practice. Place the "stones" around the room. Have children take off their shoes and "cross the river" by stepping on and reading the stones. If they cannot read a word, they "fall in and have to go home to change." When most can cross with ease, add new words from Book 18, such as *now, how, wow,* and *brown.* Read the word *now* for the children by blending *n* onto the /ow/ sound. Explain that sometimes *ow* says /ow/ as if it is hurt. Have children use this information to read *now, how, wow,* and *brown.* Intermingle these *ow* stepping stones with the others, and begin the game again.

NEW WORDS

Focus-Skill Words
chews
news
out
pouts
brown
how
now
wow

Sight Words
does
girls
their

Story Words
drives
gumball
upset

Prior to this lesson, children should have been working with activities suggested for Book 17 to build phonemic awareness, letter/sound correspondence, and blending skills. These activities should have been extended to introduce *ew, ou,* and *ow* letter/sound correspondences.

Book 18 Rhythmic Chant
To Gumball Pond
(to the tune of "Here We Go Looby Loo")

Pom-Pom hops in the cage.
Mom gets in the **brown** van.
Jan and Kate jump in the back seat,
and Gus <u>drives</u> the huge van.

Out to <u>Gumball</u> Pond—**Now!**
Out to <u>Gumball</u> Pond—**Wow!**
The van is in fog, the <u>girls</u> are <u>upset</u>,
but Pom-Pom naps in the van.

Oh …
Pom-Pom hops in the cage.
Mom gets in the **brown** van.
Jan and Kate jump in the back seat,
and Gus <u>drives</u> the huge van.

(Chant reproducible on page 113)

❶ Read *To Gumball Pond* to the children. Point to each word, and read slowly as children follow top to bottom, left to right.

❷ Read the chant again rhythmically, pointing to each word. Have children clap a steady beat as you read.

❸ Sing the chant to the tune of "Here We Go Looby Loo." Highlight the words *brown, out, now,* and *wow.* Read these words and have children read them back to you.

4 **Phonemic Awareness Strategy:** Ask children to listen to the words *pout, out, now,* and *wow.* Ask them what common sound pattern they hear in all of the words.

5 **Letter/Word Awareness Strategy:** Write the word pairs *out/pout* and *now/wow* with magnetic letters on an overhead projector. Have children examine the word pairs to find common letter patterns. Have children indicate patterns they find by having them "walk the words" on the wall and touch the common parts. Read each word pair. Say *In both pairs, we hear the "ow" sound.* Lead children to conclude that sometimes *ou* says /ow/ and sometimes *ow* says /ow/.

❻ Display the chart of *To Gumball Pond.* Point-track the words as children sing the chant to the tune of "Here We Go Looby Loo."

READ

When children have had sufficient practice with the rhythmic chant; recognize most new sight words; and seem confident with the suggested phonemic, letter/word awareness, and blending activities, they are ready to read Book 18.

1 Hold up *Out to Gumball Pond*. Ask open-ended questions such as *What do you notice on the front cover of our book?* and *What do you think our story will be about?* Identify the title, author, and illustrator.

2 Have children read the story silently (or as quietly as possible). Observe as the children read to be sure all are on task reading.

3 Have children reread the story with you in unison. Slowly read the book page by page. Note which children are able to keep up with the reading and which children seem to need more time.

4 Have children pair off and read simultaneously to each other in a low voice as you monitor their progress.

5 **Metacognitive Coaching Strategy:** Model reading for information as you reread the book together. Ask children to read until they get to the part where a problem occurs, the part that tells how the characters react to the problem, the part that tells if and how the problem is solved, and the part that tells how the story ends.

6 After the last reading, ask children to talk about the problem, the characters' reactions to the problem, the solution, and the end of the story. Ask *Would you like to go to Gumball Pond?*

REVIEW

Be the Word

Have two children link arms closely and say *ow*. Alternate other children as the beginning sound of a word, and have them blend their letters with *ow* to say *cow, how, now, wow,* and *pow*. Have them do this first without print cues. Later, have children hold letter cards and blend the letters with *ow* to form words. Repeat this activity to work with the *ew* and *ou* vowel teams and words such as *chew, new, out,* and *pout*.

Music Center

Place paper copies of the rhythmic chant *(To Gumball Pond)* and an instrumental version of "Here We Go Looby Loo" in the center. Invite children to read the chant and sing along with the music.

Overhead Projector Center

Place a large basket of magnetic letters or letter cards at the center. Invite children to reread the book *Out to Gumball Pond* and rewrite words and phrases from the story with the magnetic letters or letter cards.

Library Center

Place a large assortment of alphabet books in the center for children to read and review short and long vowels. Challenge them to find items on the pages that begin with or contain short and long *a, e, i, o,* and *u.*

Alphabet/Word Study Center

Provide cow-shaped cutouts at the center. Invite children to make their own *-ow* word-family charts. Have children write *cow, how, now, wow,* and *brown* on the cow cutouts and practice reading them.

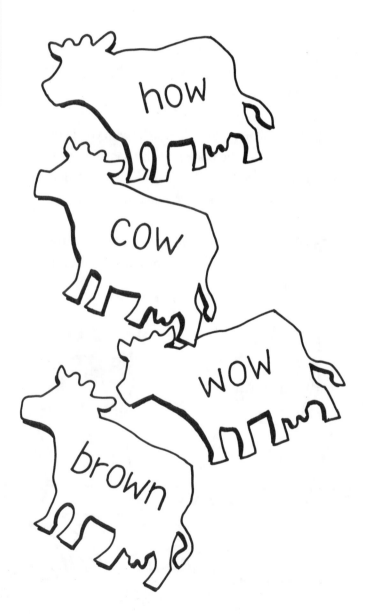

To Gumball Pond

(to the tune of "Here We Go Looby Loo")

Pom-Pom hops in the cage.
Mom gets in the brown van.
Jan and Kate jump in the back seat,
and Gus drives the huge van.

Out to Gumball Pond—Now!
Out to Gumball Pond—Wow!
The van is in fog, the girls are upset,
but Pom-Pom naps in the van.

Oh . . .
Pom-Pom hops in the cage.
Mom gets in the brown van.
Jan and Kate jump in the back seat,
and Gus drives the huge van.

19 Splish, Splash

FOCUS SKILLS 3-letter blends: str, spl, and scr

TRANSITION FROM BOOK 18 TO BOOK 19

Word Bag

Have each child in the group cut a wave pattern in the top of a lunch sack (blue, if available) and label the sack *Word Bag*. Create cutouts of beach-themed items such as shells, crabs, and boats. Write focus-skill, sight, and story words from Books 18 and 19 on the cutouts. Play ocean music as a background, and have children place the cutouts facedown, fish for a word, read it, and drop it in their Word Bag. Any words the child cannot read must be "thrown back" into the pile for another child to fish. After familiar words are practiced, display cutouts with the words *stretch, string, splash, splish, splits,* and *scream*. Demonstrate slowly how to blend all three beginning sounds onto the vowel sound and then onto the ending sound(s). Fish for each word again, read it quickly, have children read it, and place the new words into the "ocean" of words. Continue the game until all new words are properly "caught," read, and placed into a child's Word Bag.

NEW WORDS

Focus-Skill Words
Stream
stretch
string
splash
splish
splits
Scrappy
scream
screams

Sight Words
learns
move
watch

Story Words
arms
scared

READY

Prior to this lesson, children should have been working with activities suggested for Book 18 to build phonemic awareness, letter/sound correspondence, and blending skills. These activities should have been extended to introduce three-letter blends *str*, *spl*, and *scr*.

Book 19 Rhythmic Chant

Splish and Splash

(to the tune of "London Bridge Is Falling Down")

At the beach we **string** the shells,
string the shells,
string the shells.
And at the beach we <u>watch</u> the kids
do **splits** in the sand.

Into the waves we **stretch** and **scream,**
stretch and **scream,**
stretch and **scream.**
Into the waves we **splish** and **splash**
and <u>learn</u> how to swim.

(Chant reproducible on page 117)

❶ Read *Splish and Splash* to the children. Point to each word, and read slowly as children follow top to bottom, left to right.

❷ Read the chant again rhythmically, pointing to each word. Have children pretend to swim to the beat of the words as they read with you.

❸ Sing the chant to the tune of "London Bridge Is Falling Down."

❹ Point to the words, and have children sing the chant.

5 **Phonemic Awareness Strategy:** Say the words *splish* and *splash*. Ask children to describe how the words sound the same and how they sound different.

6 **Letter/Word Awareness Strategy:** Highlight on the chart the following phrases one at a time and have children dramatize what they mean: *string the shells, do splits, stretch and scream,* and *splish and splash.* Have children use different-color markers to circle all the *str* words, underline the *spl* words, and box off the *scr* words.

7 **Blending Strategy:** Write the words *splish* and *splash* in large lowercase letters. Model "Slo-Mo Blending" by slowly blending each sound of the beginning blend to create the blended sound, attaching it to the vowel, and then blending it onto the final digraph.

❽ Display the chart of *Splish and Splash.* Point-track as children sing the chant to the tune of "London Bridge Is Falling Down."

READ

When children have had sufficient practice with the rhythmic chant; recognize most new sight words; and seem confident with the suggested phonemic, letter/word awareness, and blending activities, they are ready to read Book 19.

❶ Hold up *Splish, Splash.* Ask open-ended questions such as *What do you notice on the front cover of our book?* and *What do you think our story will be about?* Identify the title, author, and illustrator.

❷ Distribute children's books. Ask children to read the story silently (or as quietly as possible). Observe their reading. Assist children who seem to be having difficulty decoding words.

3 **Metacognitive Coaching Strategy—**
Reading for Meaning: Read the first page of text aloud to the children. Ask *Did we find out who the story is about on this page? Who is it? What else did we learn on this page?* Move on page by page, reading to the children and pausing to ask them what they learned about the characters or the story on that page.

4 Read the book again slowly, and have children read with you.

5 Have children read independently in a soft voice. Move around the group, listen, and observe children's progress with decoding words and recognizing sight words.

Reading by Analogy
Write the new word *coach* on a chart. Under it, write the word *boat*. Under *boat,* write the word *chat*. Tell children that to read the top word, they could think about parts of words they do know to help them decode this word. Point out that the top word has *oa* in it, just like the familiar word *boat*. Ask students to identify the sound made by *oa* in *boat,* and explain that the *oa* in the top word makes the same sound. Remind children that they know that *c* says /k/ and *oa* says /o/, so they only need to find out the last sound. Point out that *chat* starts with *ch* and says /ch/ and that the word you are trying to read ends with /ch/. Guide the children to put the pieces together to read /c/ /oa/ /ch/ (say each part slowly). Blend the parts together, and say *coach*. Tell children that they only need to use this strategy on words they do not recognize quickly. Remind them that to read a new word they should look for parts of the word that look like parts of familiar words.

Music Center
Place in the music center the ocean music tape, the word bags, and the cutouts from the Transition section so children can listen to the music, practice reading words, and play the game "Word Bag."

Chart Center
Place the rhythmic chant *(Splish and Splash)* in the center. Invite one child to point to the words while others sing the chant and dramatize the word meanings.

Alphabet/Word Study Center
Place markers, copies of *Splish, Splash,* and photocopies of the rhythmic chant in the center. Invite children to read *Splish, Splash* and mark words in the chant that are the same as words in the book. (Be sure children mark only on the chant and not in the book.)

Splish and Splash

(to the tune of "London Bridge Is Falling Down")

At the beach we string the shells,
string the shells,
string the shells.
And at the beach we watch the kids
do splits in the sand.

Into the waves we stretch and scream,
stretch and scream,
stretch and scream.
Into the waves we splish and splash
and learn how to swim.

20 Barney Bear's Party

FOCUS SKILLS r-controlled vowels

TRANSITION FROM
BOOK 19 TO BOOK 20

Book Boxes

Gather several gift boxes and put a bow on each one. Cut long paper strips equal to or narrower than the width of the boxes and accordion-fold the strips. (Cut one strip for each box.) Write a focus-skill or story word from Book 19 on each of the folded segments, leaving blank the segment at the far right end. Glue the blank segment of each paper strip into the bottom of a separate box. Invite children to select a box, open the "gift of words," and read the words in the box. Repeat this activity for the focus-skill, sight, and story words in Book 20. Read the words to the children first, and then have them read the words to you. Point out how in the focus-skill words the *r* sound changes the vowel's sound. (Note: Use this as an awareness session for *r*-controlled vowels rather than a direct teaching or mastery session.)

NEW WORDS

Focus-Skill Words

B**ar**ney	h**ere**
B**ar**ney's	l**ater**
B**ear**	monst**er**s
B**ear**'s	**over**
b**ir**d	p**ar**ty
b**ir**thday	p**ur**ple
c**ar**	sh**ir**t
f**ar**	s**ur**prise
f**ar**m	y**ar**d
f**ir**st	y**ear**

Sight Words

asked
once
open

Story Words

gifts
Momma
played

Prior to this lesson, children should have been working with activities suggested for Book 19 to build phonemic awareness, letter/sound correspondence, and blending skills. These activities should have been extended to introduce *r*-controlled vowels' letter/sound correspondences.

Book 20 Rhythmic Chant
Barney's Birthday Chant
(to the tune of "An Old-Fashioned Birthday Song," or as a rhythmic chant)

Today is **Barney Bear's birthday,
birthday, birthday.**
Today is **Barney Bear's birthday.
Surprise! Surprise** for me!

Barney <u>opens</u> a toy **bird,**
a **farm** set, a race **car.**
Barney <u>opens</u> a **purple shirt,**
has punch, and eats sweet treats.

(Chant reproducible on page 122)

1 Read *Barney's Birthday Chant* to the children. Point to each word, and read slowly as children follow top to bottom, left to right.

2 Read the chant again. Ask children to listen for Barney's gifts and for what was served at his party.

3 Have volunteers point to and underline the words describing Barney's gifts. Ask other children to point to and circle the words describing Barney's party foods.

4 As a group, reread the underlined and circled words.

5 Have children read the chant as you point to each word.

6 Sing the chant to the tune of "An Old-Fashioned Birthday Song." (You can also tap a rhythmic beat and chant the rhyme instead of singing it.)

7 Sing or chant the song again in unison with the children.

8 **Phonemic Awareness Strategy:** Ask children to listen to the words *car, far, bar, jar, star,* and *tar.* Ask children what they notice about the sounds in each of the words.

9 **Letter/Word Awareness Strategy:** Write the words *car, far, bar, jar, star,* and *tar.* Ask children which letters make the *r*-controlled vowel sound in each word.

10 **Blending Strategy:** Have children read the words *car, far, bar, jar, star,* and *tar.* Have children extend their left arm as they say the beginning sound, extend their right arm as they say the phonogram *(-ar),* and pull both arms back as they read the word.

11 Display the chart of *Barney's Birthday Chant.* Point-track and read rhythmically or sing as children join in.

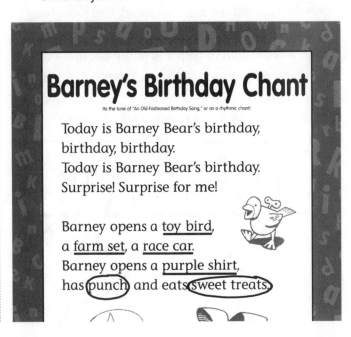

When children have had sufficient practice with the rhythmic chant; recognize most new sight words; and seem confident with the suggested phonemic, letter/word awareness, and blending activities, they are ready to read Book 20.

1 Hold up *Barney Bear's Party*. Ask open-ended questions such as *What do you notice on the front cover of our book?* and *What do you think our story will be about?* Identify the title, author, and illustrator.

2 Distribute children's books. Have children quietly read with you as you read aloud.

3 Call attention to the sight words *asked, once,* and *open.* Review these with children and have them locate the words in the story.

4 Reread the story to the children two pages at a time. Have children read the same two pages back to you. Notice which words seem to give the children difficulty.

5 **Metacognitive Coaching Strategy:** Reread the first two pages, and model for children how to decode the words *Momma* and *soon.* Ask children to help you figure out these words by pretending you do not know them. For example, you might box off with your fingers the word *Mom* in *Momma* and say to the children *Here is a word I*

know—Mom. Then, show the *ma* ending and blend the *m* and short *a* sounds together. Finally, slowly say the two word "chunks" *(Mom* and *ma)* before quickly blending them together and exclaiming that the word must be *Momma*.

6 Read the story again slowly, and have children read with you.

7 Have children read independently in a soft voice. Move around the group, listen, and observe children's progress with decoding words and recognizing sight words.

Writing Phonograms
Duplicate the Read-a-Ladder reproducible (page 150). Write *-ar* at the bottom of the ladder. Have children write their way up the ladder as you call out *-ar* words such as *bar, car, far, jar, star,* and *tar.*

Blending Sounds

After having children write up the ladder, have them read their way up the ladder by blending beginning sound(s) onto the *r*-controlled *-ar* phonogram.

Big Book Center

Write the text of *Barney Bear's Party* on large sheets of paper and place them in the center. Invite children to illustrate each page to match the text. When finished, bind the pages together to make a big book. Invite children to read their own version of *Barney Bear's Party*.

Library Center

Place copies of Books 16–20 in the library center for children to read and reread to partners, to an older book buddy, or silently to themselves.

Alphabet/Word Study Center

Place Book Boxes from the Transition section in the center so children can practice their word work and fluent word recognition.

Barney's Birthday Chant

(to the tune of "An Old-Fashioned Birthday Song," or as a rhythmic chant)

Today is Barney Bear's birthday,
birthday, birthday.
Today is Barney Bear's birthday.
Surprise! Surprise for me!

Barney opens a toy bird,
a farm set, a race car.
Barney opens a purple shirt,
has punch, and eats sweet treats.

[21] The Rainy Day Band

FOCUS SKILLS contractions

TRANSITION FROM
BOOK 20 TO BOOK 21

Rainy Day Fun

Cut large raindrops from blue construction paper. Label these with the following words from Books 20 and 21: *first, over, yard, year, party, bird, car, farm, for,* and *forks*. Place the raindrops in a bucket or box, and "shower" the children with raindrops. Invite each child to pick up one raindrop and read it. After all the raindrops have been read once, affix them to an umbrella, open the umbrella, twirl it slowly, and have children reread all of the raindrops.

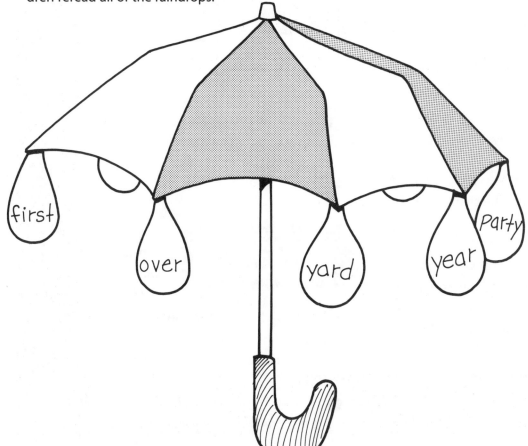

NEW WORDS

Focus-Skill Words
he'll
I'll
it's
let's
we'll
we're
you'll

Sight Words
family
family's
great
two

Story Words
begin
cooking
raining
rainy
ready
roasting
tuned

Prior to this lesson, children should have been working with activities suggested for Book 20 to build phonemic awareness, letter/sound correspondence, and blending skills. These activities should have been extended to introduce the concept of contractions.

Book 21 Rhythmic Chant
Rain, Rain, Go Away

Rain, rain, go away.
The <u>family</u> wants to play today.
<u>Ready</u>, one, <u>two</u>, **let's** <u>begin</u>.
We're all <u>tuned</u> up.
We'll play to the end!

(Chant reproducible on page 126)

❶ Read *Rain, Rain, Go Away* to the children. Point to each word, and read slowly as children follow top to bottom, left to right.

❷ Read the chant again rhythmically, pointing to each word as children follow and read with you.

❸ Have children read the chant to you as you point-track the words.

❹ Have children match word cards for *family, ready, one, two, begin,* and *tuned* to the chant. Reread the words together.

❺ Call children's attention to the words *We're* and *We'll.* Ask if they know what each of these words means. Lead them to determine that *We're* means *We are* and *We'll* means *We will.*

6 **Phonemic Awareness Strategy:**
Ask children to listen to the words *rain, rainy,* and *raining* to determine how the words are

different. Did they notice the difference in the ending of the words? (This activity provides awareness for Book 23's focus skill of simple word endings. It is important that children can hear these endings before actually working with them in print.)

7 **Letter/Word Awareness Strategy—**
Fold the Words: Write the following phrases on separate sentence strips: *he will, I will, it is, let us, we will, we are,* and *you will.* Have children read each sentence strip. In front of the children, crease and fold each strip over the letters that are removed to form the contraction. Attach to a paper clip a small self-adhesive note upon which an apostrophe is drawn. Clip the note to the folded piece of a sentence strip to hold the strip in place. Do this for each sentence strip. When finished, have children read the contractions *he'll, I'll, it's, let's, we'll, we're,* and *you'll.*

❽ Display the chart of *Rain, Rain, Go Away.* Point-track and read the chant rhythmically with children in unison.

When children have had sufficient practice with the rhythmic chant; recognize most new sight words; and seem confident with the suggested phonemic, letter/word awareness, and blending activities, they are ready to read Book 21.

❶ Hold up *The Rainy Day Band.* Ask open-ended questions such as *What do you notice on the front* cover of our book? and *What do you think our story will be about?* Identify the title, author, and illustrator.

② Distribute children's books. Ask children to read the book in a soft voice as you watch, ready to help if they need you.

③ Ask children to read aloud with you for their second reading.

④ Have children find partners and read simultaneously to each other.

⑤ **Metacognitive Coaching Strategy:** Read the first sentence to the children. Think out loud about the contraction *it's* meaning *it is*, *raining* as a word they know with the *-ing* ending added to it, and the big word *outside* as two little words they know. Then, ask children to read on to find other words to which the *-ing* ending has been added and raise their hands when they find two more. From that point, finish rereading the story aloud together.

The Contraction Glove

Place Velcro pieces on the front lower half, the front upper half, and on the back lower half of a long glove or oven mitt. Prepare word cards with Velcro attached to the back for *he, will, I, it, is, let, us, we, are,* and *you* using the Contraction Cards reproducible (page 155). Then, prepare similar cards for *he'll, I'll, it's, let's, we're,* and *you'll.* Invite a child to attach the words *he will* to the front of the glove and the word *he'll* to the back. Have the child show the front of the glove to the group, say *he will,* and bend ("contract") his or her arm to show and read *he'll.* Repeat the process for other contractions with new volunteers.

Writing Center

Encourage children to write lyrics for songs they know. Provide rhythm band instruments to use as accompaniment. Have children read their lyrics, sing their songs, and accompany themselves in a class "reading" band.

Art Center

Have children draw scenes from *The Rainy Day Band* that depict the "kitchen band instruments." Invite children to reread the book, locate words describing these instruments, and label their pictures with the names of the instruments.

Listening Center

Place tape-recorded band music and copies of *The Rainy Day Band* in the center. Play the music in the background while children read and reread the book to themselves, to partners, or to an older book buddy.

Alphabet/Word Study Center

Place in the center the materials from The Contraction Glove activity in the Review section. Invite children to play the contraction games to reinforce earlier learning. Also, place in the center the umbrella and raindrop word cards from the Transition section so children can practice fluent reading of focus-skill, sight, and story words.

Rain, Rain, Go Away

Rain, rain, go away.

The family wants to play today.

Ready, one, two, let's begin.

We're all tuned up.

We'll play to the end!

22 Cat and Dog at the Circus

FOCUS SKILLS question words, soft c and g

TRANSITION FROM
BOOK 21 TO BOOK 22

Popcorn Reading

Bring a popcorn container from a movie theater and tape to it the Popcorn Word Cards (page 156). For one popcorn reading game, use the *Cathy, Cindy, cotton, cage, city, circus, center,* and *candy* cards. For a second game, use the *giant, goat, hug, huge, cage, gift,* and *girls* cards. As children pick a piece of "popcorn" to read, help them use familiar spelling/sound correspondences and knowledge of known words to decode the words. At the end of game one, lead children to conclude that *c* can make a hard sound as in *cat* or a soft sound as in *city.* At the end of the second game, conclude that *g* also can make a hard sound as in *goat* and *hug* or a soft sound as in *giant* and *huge.*

NEW WORDS

Focus-Skill Words

what

what's

when

where

which

who

why

ca**g**e

center

Cindy

circus

city

giant

hu**g**e

Sight Words

began

some

Story Words

candy

Cathy

cotton

popcorn

ticket

tickets

Prior to this lesson, children should have been working with activities suggested for Book 21 to build phonemic awareness, letter/sound correspondence, and blending skills. These activities should have been extended to introduce question words and soft *c* and *g* letter/sound correspondences.

Book 22 Rhythmic Chant
The City Circus Show
(to the tune of "Alexander's Ragtime Band," or as a rhythmic chant)

Come on with Cat, come on with Dog
to the **city circus** show.
Buy a <u>ticket</u>. Eat <u>cotton candy</u>.
Get ready, it's time to go.

Well you can watch **what's** going on
in the **center circus** ring.
See a **giant** clown in a cute car do his thing.

So, come on with Cat, come on with Dog
to the **city circus** show.

(Chant reproducible on page 131)

❶ Read *The City Circus Show* to the children. Point to each word, and read slowly as children follow top to bottom, left to right.

❷ Read the chant again rhythmically, pointing to each word as children read with you.

❸ Sing the chant to the tune of "Alexander's Ragtime Band."

❹ Point to the words, and have children sing with you.

5 **Phonemic Awareness Strategy:**
Ask children to listen to the following words: *city, circus,* and *center.* Ask children what sound starts these words. Ask the same question about the words *clown, cat, cute,* and *car.*

6 **Letter/Word Awareness Strategy:**
Write the words *city, circus,* and *center* in a column on a chalkboard or chart paper. Write in another column *clown, cat, cute,* and *car.* Have a volunteer trace with a marker each word's beginning letter. Ask *What letter starts all of these words? What do you notice when I say the words in the first column. What sound does* c *make? What sound does* c *make in the words in the second column?* Lead children to conclude that *c* sometimes makes a soft sound and sometimes makes a hard sound.

❼ Display the chart of *The City Circus Show.* Point-track the words and sing the chant in unison.

READ

When children have had sufficient practice with the rhythmic chant; recognize most new sight words; and seem confident with the suggested phonemic, letter/word awareness, and blending activities, they are ready to read Book 22.

❶ Hold up *Cat and Dog at the Circus.* Ask open-ended questions such as *What do you notice on the front cover of our book?* and *What do you think our story will be about?* Identify the title, author, and illustrator.

❷ Distribute children's books. Ask children to read the book silently (or as quietly as possible).

❸ Ask children to read aloud with you for their second reading.

▲4 **Metacognitive Coaching Strategy—Question the Author:** Create and distribute question-word necklaces made from sentence strips and ribbon. Have each of six children wear one question word. Ask the *Who?* child *Who are the characters in this story?* Ask each child wearing a question word an appropriate question such as *What is the story about? Where does the story take place? When does the story take place? Why did Cat and Dog use a scope? Which thing at the circus did Cat see last in the scope?* Have the children read the part from the story that answers the question or answer the question in his or her own words. This game helps children think about the author's intentions for the story and develop a sense of personal meaning about the story.

❺ Have children quietly read independently as you monitor and assess their progress.

REVIEW

The Question Game

Create an overhead transparency of the Interview reproducible (page 157). Interview one child at a time in front of the group, and record his or her responses. Model how you figure out the spelling for each word you write. (For example, recall words you know, recall sound/spelling correspondences, or say the word and listen for sounds in it.) When the interviews are finished, have the children read the question words each time and you read the recorded responses. Later, at center time, children will practice this process independently.

Writing Center

Encourage children to act as reporters and interview classmates or older book buddies. Make copies of the Interview reproducible (page 157). Have children use their knowledge of phonics and word awareness to read the question words during the interview and record simple responses to questions such as

What is your name?
When is your birthday?
Where do you live?
Who is your favorite teacher?
Why do you come to school?
Which book do you like best?

Art Center

Have children draw a picture of the person they interviewed, cut it out, label it with the person's full name, and attach it to the interview form.

Listening Center

Place in the listening center recorded songs about clowns, the circus, tigers, lions, and other circus-related topics. Invite children to listen to a song and write circus words on a sheet of pink, cotton candy-shaped paper.

Library Center

Place in the library center several stories from the *Dr. Maggie's Phonics Readers* series, including *Cat and Dog at the Circus* and the question-word necklaces used in the Read section, Step 4. Invite children to wear the necklaces as one child reads a story to them. Have them read their question word and create and answer questions beginning with that word based on their knowledge of the story.

Alphabet/Word Study Center

Place in the center photocopies of the rhythmic chant *(The City Circus Show)* and baskets of letter cards or magnetic letters. Invite children to read the chant, select words, and then make the words with the letter cards or magnetic letters. Have them record on paper strips the words they make to take home, read, and review. Also, place the popcorn container and popcorn word notes in the center so children can practice the "Popcorn Reading" game (see Transition section).

The City Circus Show

(to the tune of "Alexander's Ragtime Band," or as a rhythmic chant)

Come on with Cat, come on with Dog
to the city circus show.
Buy a ticket. Eat cotton candy.
Get ready, it's time to go.

Well you can watch what's going on
in the center circus ring.
See a giant clown in a cute car do his thing.

So, come on with Cat, come on with Dog
to the city circus show.

23 Jo Jo in Outer Space

FOCUS SKILLS simple word endings: -er, -ed, -ly, -y

TRANSITION FROM
BOOK 22 TO BOOK 23

Word Launch

Cut out space-related shapes such as suns, moons, spaceships, or stars. Write on these cutouts the words *deep, deeper, out, outer, ask, asked, look, looked, move, moved, pull, pulled, save, saved, want, wanted, zoom, zoomed, slow,* and *slowly.* Place the cutouts facedown on a chair labeled *Launching Pad.* Select a word and read it to the children. If it is a word without an ending (*-er, -ed, -ly,* or *-y*), pretend it is a "misfire" and set it aside. Select another word. If it has an ending, tell children it has "launching power." Pretend to launch the word into outer space and attach it to a piece of dark paper (blue or black). After your initial modeling, have children continue playing the game until all launching power words have been attached to the dark paper and all others are placed in the misfire pile. Tell children that it takes more power to read a word with an added ending because you have to decode the word, identify the ending, and add the ending to the word.

NEW WORDS

Focus-Skill Words

aft**er**

deep**er**

out**er**

ask**ed**

look**ed**

mov**ed**

pull**ed**

sav**ed**

want**ed**

zoom**ed**

slow**ly**

angr**y**

scar**y**

ver**y**

Sight Words

talk

want

Story Words

front

please

READY

Prior to this lesson, children should have been working with activities suggested for Book 22 to build phonemic awareness, letter/sound correspondence, and blending skills. These activities should have been extended to introduce simple word endings -er, -ed, -ly, and -y.

Book 23 Rhythmic Chant
Out to Outer Space
(to the tune of "The Farmer in the Dell")

Out to **outer** space,
deep and **deeper** we go.
We **asked** the man in the moon to smile,
then **after** we **zoomed** back home!

(Chant reproducible on page 135)

❶ Read *Out to Outer Space* to the children. Point to each word, and read slowly as children follow top to bottom, left to right.

❷ Sing the chant to the tune of "The Farmer in the Dell" as you track the words.

❸ Have children sing the chant to you as you track the words.

4 **Phonemic Awareness Strategy:** Ask children to listen to pairs of words such as *out* and *outer* to determine where they are different. Ask them what they notice about the endings of the words.

5 **Letter/Word Awareness Strategy:** Underline *Out* in the first line of the chant. Ask children to find this word again in the same line. Ask what they notice about the word the second time it appears in the sentence. Lead them to realize it is the same word, but it has additional letters as an ending.

Ask them to identify the ending. Repeat the activity for *deep* in the second line. Then, write the words *ask* and *zoom* and have children find them in the third and fourth lines. Challenge children to identify the ending that has been added to the root word.

READ

When children have had sufficient practice with the rhythmic chant; recognize most new sight words; and seem confident with the suggested phonemic, letter/word awareness, and blending activities, they are ready to read Book 23.

❶ Hold up *Jo Jo in Outer Space*. Ask open-ended questions such as *What do you notice on the front cover of our book?* and *What do you think our story will be about?* Identify the title, author, and illustrator.

❷ Distribute children's books. Ask them to read the book silently (or as quietly as possible).

❸ Ask children to read aloud with you for their second reading.

4 **Metacognitive Coaching Strategy—Recalling Prior Knowledge:** Ask children to look for and name familiar characters in this story. Ask *In which book did we read about these characters before?* Display several previous books, and have children select the correct title.

5 Ask several volunteers to reread aloud the original story (Book 15: *The Little Green Man Visits Pine Cone Cove*) to the group.

6 Ask other volunteers to read aloud the new story to the group.

7 Talk about similarities and differences in the two stories. Discuss the characters, setting, problem (plot), events, and conclusion. Create as a class a Venn diagram that compares and contrasts the two stories.

 **Word Detectives**

Write on the left side of a two-column chart the words *by, my, sly, fry,* and *try.* On the right side, write the words *very, scary, angry,* and *slowly.* Have volunteers highlight with a marker the last letter in each of the words on both sides. Ask children what they notice about these words. Have children read the left column of words. Ask *In each word, what sound does* y *at the end make?* Do the same with the right column. Ask what the *y* says at the end of those words. Reread the first column, and clap the syllables. Reread the second column, and clap the syllables. Ask *Which column has one-syllable words? Which column has two-syllable words? What do we notice in these two columns about the* y *sound?* Lead children to observe that the -*y* ending in the one-syllable words makes a long *i* sound, while the same ending in two-syllable words makes a long *e* sound.

 **Writing Center**

Invite children to think about Jo Jo and the little green man and create a new adventure for them. Ask older book buddies to help younger children use their phonics knowledge to write their new adventure.

Art Center

Invite children to illustrate Jo Jo and the little green man's new adventure using watercolors, markers, or crayons. Have them use their phonics and word knowledge to label items in the scene with correct spelling.

Library Center

Place copies of Books 15 and 23 in the library center. Invite children to read them with a partner and make their own comparisons between the stories.

Out to Outer Space

(to the tune of "The Farmer in the Dell")

Out to outer space,
deep and deeper we go.
We asked the man in the moon to smile,
then after we zoomed back home!

Dr. Maggie's Phonics Resource Guide © 1999 Creative Teaching Press

Riddle and Rhyme with Apron Annie

FOCUS SKILLS rhyming words, 2-syllable words

TRANSITION FROM
BOOK 23 TO BOOK 24

Rhyme Time Flip Books
Duplicate the Rhyme Time Flip Books reproducibles (pages 158–159) and use them to make rhyming word books. Flip the rhyming word book for the *-all* phonogram, and have children use familiar spelling/sound patterns and their knowledge of blends to read *ball, mall, tall, fall,* and *hall.* Repeat this process with the *-ay* phonogram book and the *-ook* phonogram book. Ask children if they can think of other words that could go in each book.

NEW WORDS

Focus-Skill Words
b**all**, f**all**, h**all**,
   sm**all**, st**all**
b**ay**, cl**ay**, m**ay**, pl**ay**,
   st**ay**, tr**ay**,
b**ook**, br**ook**, c**ook**,
   l**ook**, sh**ook**,
began
going
later
pockets

Sight Words
because
school
words

Story Words
Annie
apron
bounce
guess
rhyme
riddle
roll

Prior to this lesson, children should have been working with activities suggested for Book 23 to build phonemic awareness, letter/sound correspondence, and blending skills. These activities should have been extended to introduce rhyming and two-syllable words.

Book 24 Rhythmic Chant
Rhyme the Words Time

<u>Riddle</u>, <u>riddle</u>,
<u>riddle</u>, and <u>rhyme</u>.
It's time. It's time.
It's <u>rhyme</u> the <u>words</u> time.

Can you <u>guess</u>
my <u>riddle</u> today?
<u>Guess</u> the <u>riddle</u>
if you want to **play.**

<u>Riddle</u>, <u>riddle</u>,
<u>riddle</u>, and <u>rhyme</u>.
It's time. It's time.
It's <u>rhyme</u> the words time.

(Chant reproducible on page 140)

1 Read *Rhyme the Words Time* to the children. Point to each word, and read slowly as children follow top to bottom, left to right.

2 Read the chant again rhythmically, pointing to each word as children follow and read with you.

3 Have children read the chant to you as you track the words.

4 Have children match to the text word cards for *riddle, rhyme, guess,* and *words.* Read the cards. Circle each of these target words.

5 Reread the chant with the children, paying special attention to the target words.

6 **Phonemic Awareness Strategy:**
Ask children to listen to the words *riddle* and *rhyme.* Ask what they notice about the beginning sounds and the beats (syllables) of the words. Clap the syllables of *rhyme,* and ask children to name how many beats they heard. Repeat for *riddle.* Explain how some words have one beat or syllable, other words have two, and some have many more. Ask children to stand up if they have a "one-beat" name. Count those children. Repeat for children with "two-beat" names. Have children say their classmates' names and clap the beats. (Tell the class you will talk about children with three or more syllables in their names later.)

7 **Letter/Word Awareness Strategy:**
On the left side of the board, write the word *rhyme* and put a numeral 1 above it. Write the word *riddle* on the right side of the board and put a numeral 2 above it. Have children reread the chant *Rhyme the Words Time* and decide if each word has one or two syllables. Write each word under the appropriate heading.

8 Display the chant and read it rhythmically one more time with the children in unison.

**READ**

When children have had sufficient practice with the rhythmic chant; recognize most new sight words; and seem confident with the suggested phonemic, letter/word awareness, and blending activities, they are ready to read Book 24.

1 Hold up *Riddle and Rhyme with Apron Annie*. Ask open-ended questions such as *What do you notice on the front cover of our book?* and *What do you think our story will be about?* Identify the title, author, and illustrator.

2 Distribute children's books. Ask children to read the book with you as you slowly read page by page.

3 Write these words on a chart and review them with the children one at a time: *apron, Annie, bounce, guess, rhyme, riddle, roll, school, words, because,* and *going.* Ask for volunteers to read the whole word list to the group.

4 **Metacognitive Coaching Strategy:** Ask the children to read the book again, silently this time (or as quietly as possible). Remind them that some words that look longer may be two-syllable words. Advise them to look for smaller parts that they recognize and put the parts together to decode the whole word.

5 Again, ask children to read aloud with you.

**REVIEW**

Rhyming Word Wallets

Make a "word wallet" by folding a large sheet of construction paper in half lengthwise, stapling the ends, and folding it in thirds to create three pockets. Label the pockets with the three phonograms in the story (*-all, -ay,* and *-ook*). Display the word wallet for children, and read the phonograms. Invite children to suggest beginning sounds to create real or nonsense words. Write these words on separate index cards, read them, and place them in the pockets of the wallet. Make the wallet available for children to remove the cards, shuffle them, and replace them in the correct pockets.

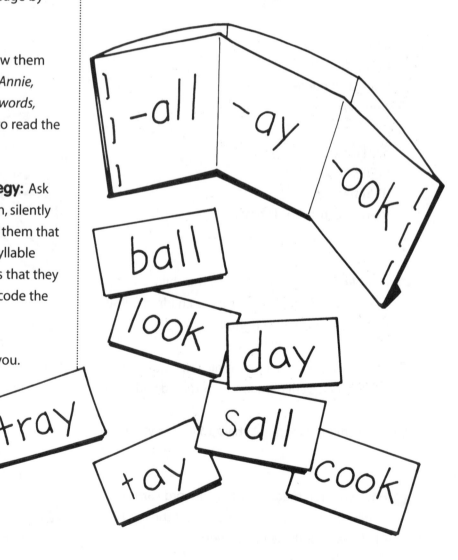

Big Book Center

Write the text for *Riddle and Rhyme with Apron Annie* on large sheets of paper and place them in the center. Invite children to illustrate the text. Then, bind the pages together to create your children's own big-book version of Apron Annie's story. Attach a cloth apron to the cover to add the finishing touch. Glue library pockets inside the pages so children can place the rhyming word lists in "Annie's pockets" on the appropriate pages.

Alphabet/Word Study Center

Place in the center the Rhyme Time Flip Books (see Transition section) so children can read and practice rhyming words independently.

Library Center

Glue library pockets to a large piece of poster board. Write at the top of index cards rhyming phonograms from *Riddle and Rhyme with Apron Annie* (i.e., *-all, -ay,* and *-ook*). (Be sure the index cards fit in the library pockets.) Place these materials in the center. Have children read the book and the rhythmic chant *(Rhyme the Words Time),* locate rhyming words, write them on the phonogram cards, and place the cards in the library pockets. Invite children to add to the phonogram cards every time they discover a new rhyming word.

Rhyme the Words Time

Riddle, riddle,
riddle, and rhyme.
It's time. It's time.
It's rhyme the words time.

Can you guess
my riddle today?
Guess the riddle
if you want to play.

Riddle, riddle,
riddle, and rhyme.
It's time. It's time.
It's rhyme the words time.

Alphabet Cards

(Page 1)

A	B	C	D	E
F	G	H	I	J
K	L	M	N	O
P	Q	R	S	T

Alphabet Cards

(Page 2)

U	V	W	X	Y
Z	a	b	c	d
e	f	g	h	i
j	k	l	m	n

Dr. Maggie's Phonics Resource Guide © 1999 Creative Teaching Press

Alphabet Cards

(Page 3)

o	p	q	r	s
t	u	v	w	x
y	z	th	ch	sh
wh	oi	oy	ow	ou

Pug the Pup

Dr. Maggie's Phonics Resource Guide © 1999 Creative Teaching Press

Spinners

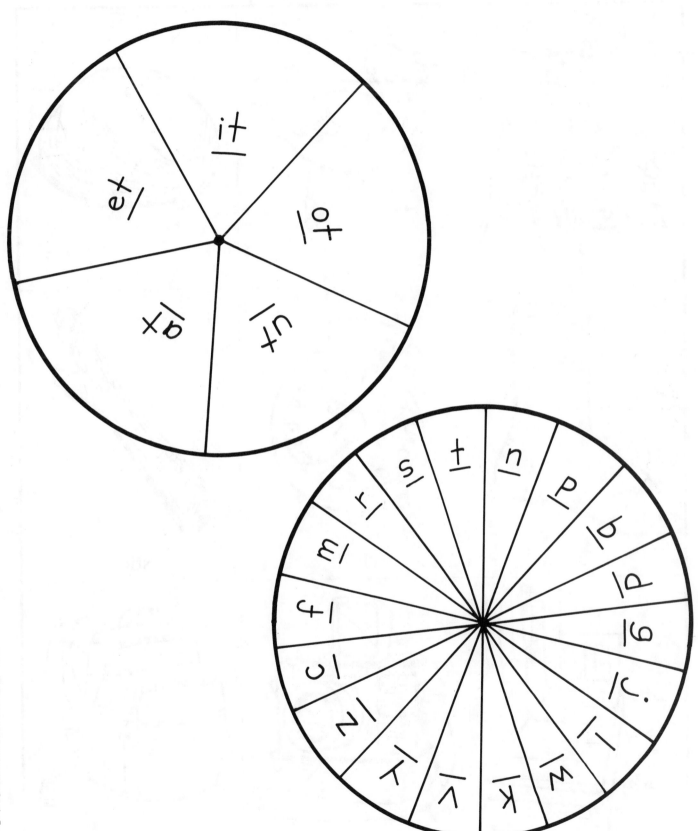

Click, Click Picture Cards

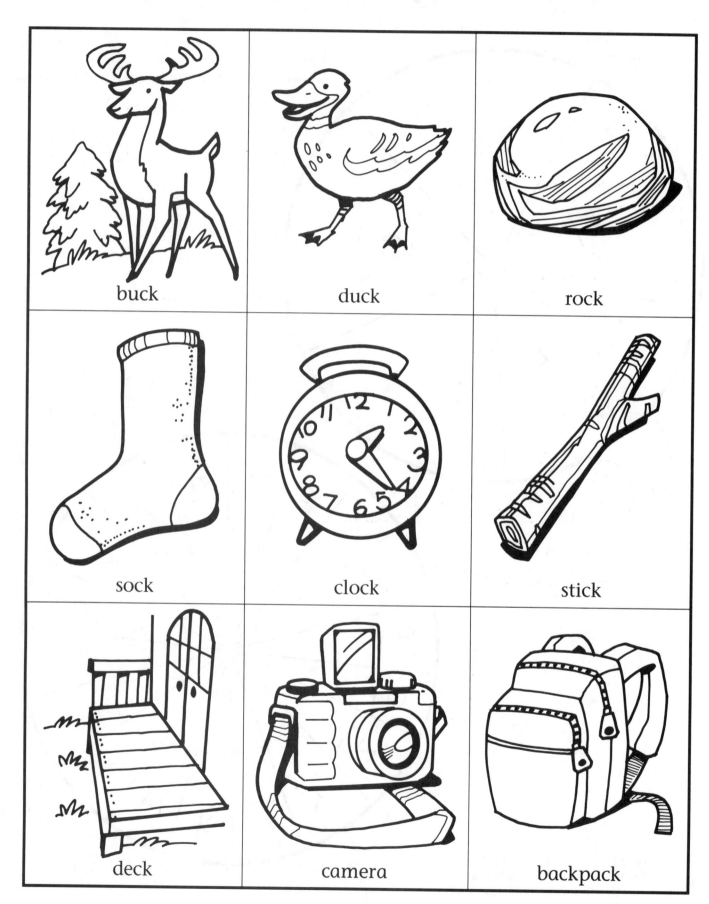

buck

duck

rock

sock

clock

stick

deck

camera

backpack

Dr. Maggie's Phonics Resource Guide © 1999 Creative Teaching Press

Scroll-a-Sound

a	e	i	o	u

Word Family: -all

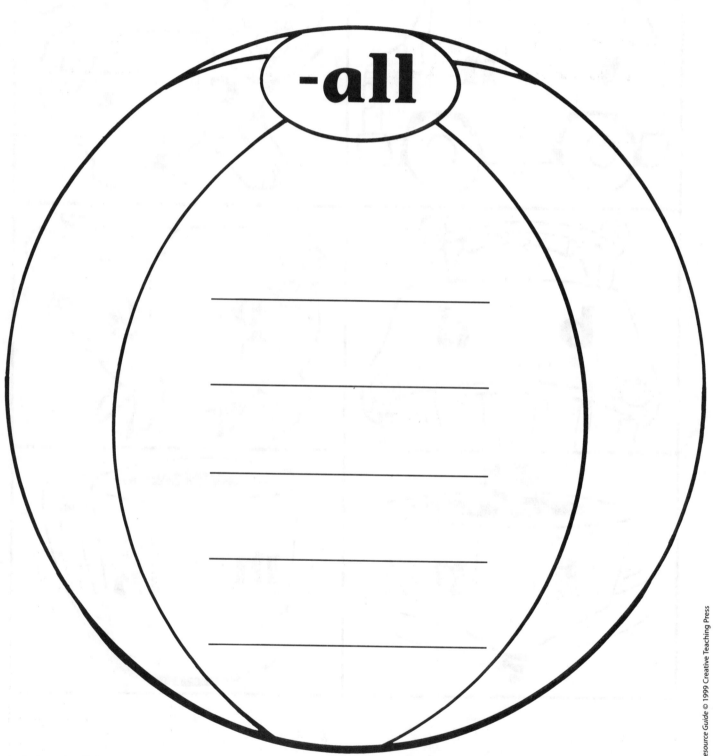

Dr. Maggie's Phonics Resource Guide © 1999 Creative Teaching Press

Word Puzzles

call ing	stay ing
pick ing	pack ing
stick ing	kick ing
yell ing	click ing
say ing	quack ing

Read-a-Ladder

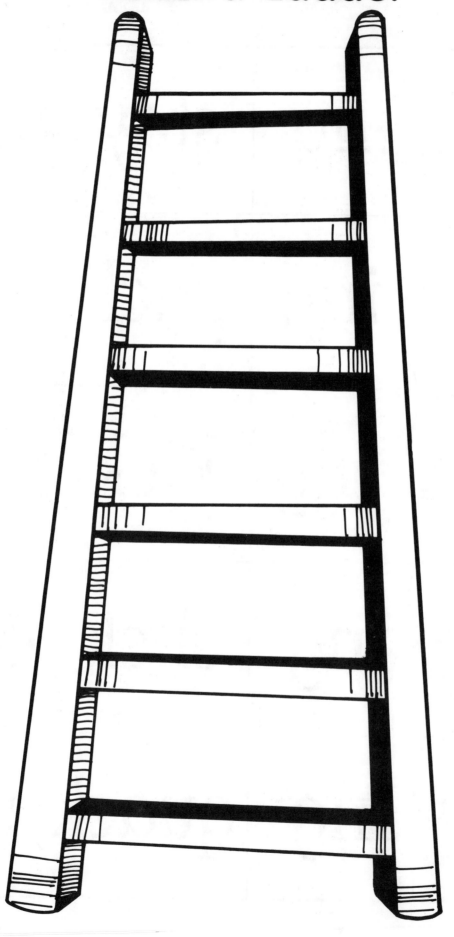

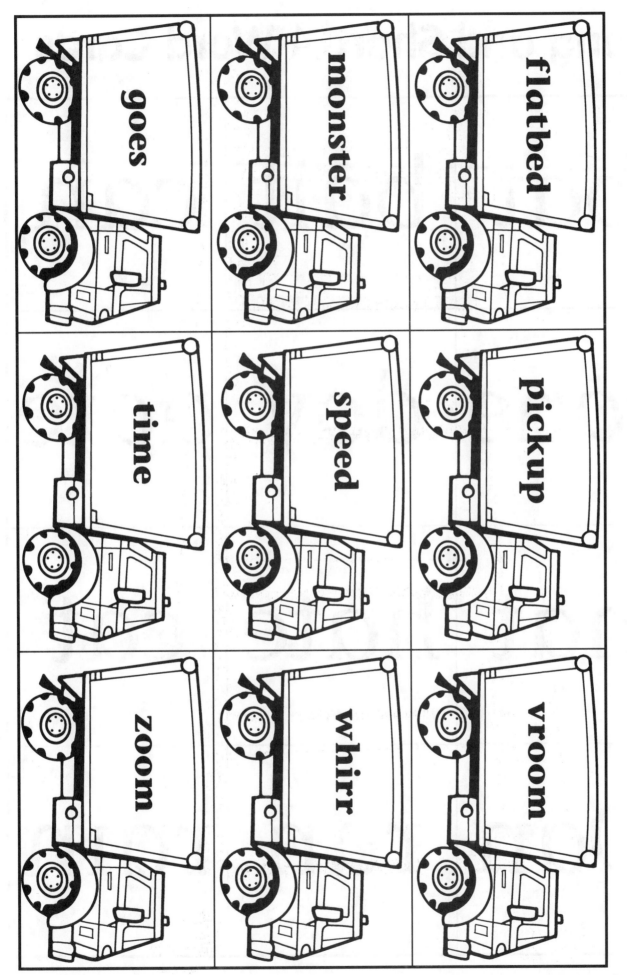

goes

monster

flatbed

time

speed

pickup

zoom

whirr

vroom

Long and Short *A* Word Cards

bat	bait	can
cane	day	date
hat	hate	cat
Dan	ran	rain

Dr. Maggie's Phonics Resource Guide © 1999 Creative Teaching Press

My Word Sort

Dr. Maggie's Phonics Resource Guide © 1999 Creative Teaching Press

Mr. Noisy and Friends

Mr. Noisy	Duke	Roy	Lucky Luke
Jules	June	Rudy	

Dr. Maggie's Phonics Resource Guide © 1999 Creative Teaching Press

Contraction Cards

he	will
is	let
are	you
it's	let's
I	it
us	we
he'll	I'll
you'll	we're

Popcorn Word Cards

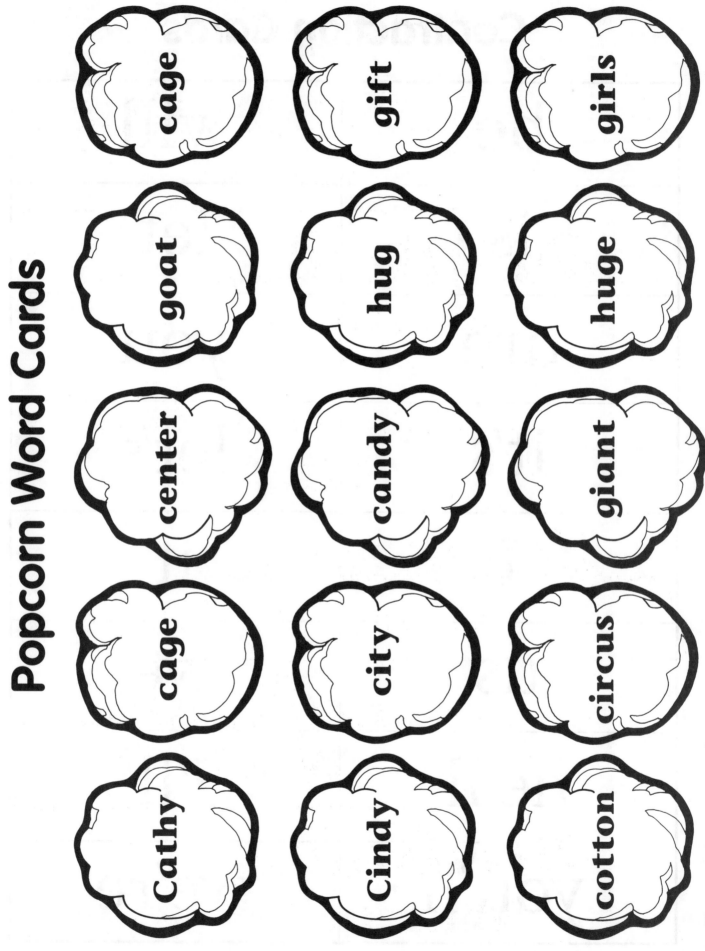

cage

gift

girls

goat

hug

huge

center

candy

giant

cage

city

circus

Cathy

Cindy

cotton

Interview

What?

When?

Where?

Who?

Why?

Which?

Rhyme Time Flip Books

(Part 1)

Cut out each word-ending box. Cut apart the letters from Part 2 and staple them in a stack in front of each word ending. Flip the letters to show the rhyming words.

_____ all

_____ ay

_____ ook

Rhyme Time Flip Books

(Part 2)

b	c	d
h	l	m
f	t	w

Bibliography

Bibliography of Research Materials

Adams, M. *Beginning to Read: Thinking and Learning about Print*. The MIT Press, 1990.

Ball, E., and B. A. Blachman. "Does Phoneme Awareness Training in Kindergarten Make a Difference in Early Word Recognition and Developmental Spelling?" *Reading Research Quarterly* 26, no. 1 (1991): 49–66.

Beck, I., and C. Juel. "The Role of Decoding in Learning to Read." *American Educator* 19, no. 2 (1995): 8, 21–25, 39–42.

Bryant, P., et al. "Rhyme, Alliteration, Phoneme Detection and Learning to Read." *Developmental Psychology* 26 (1990): 429–438.

Byrne, B., and R. Fielding-Barnsley. "Phonemic Awareness and Letter Knowledge in the Child's Acquisition of the Alphabetic Principle." *Journal of Educational Psychology* 83, no. 3 (1989): 313–321.

Cunningham, A. E. "Explicit Versus Implicit Instruction in Phonemic Awareness." *Journal of Experimental Child Psychology* 50 (1990): 429–444.

Gough, P. B., and C. Juel. "The First Stages of Word Recognition." In *Learning to Read* edited by L. Rieben and C. A. Perfetti. Erlbaum, 1991.

Griffith, P. L., and M. W. Olson. "Phonemic Awareness Helps Beginning Readers Break the Code." *The Reading Teacher* 45 (1992): 516–523.

Hatcher, P. J., C. Hulme, and A. W. Ellis. "Ameliorating Early Reading Failure by Integrating the Teaching of Reading and Phonological Skills: The Phonological Linkage Hypothesis." *Child Development* 65 (1994): 41–57.

Juel, C. "Beginning Reading." In *Handbook of Reading Research,* Vol. 2 edited by R. Barr et al. Longman, 1991.

Moats, L. C. *Spelling: Development, Disability, and Instruction.* York Press, 1995.

Stanovich, K. E. "Matthew Effects in Reading: Some Consequences of Individual Differences in the Acquisition of Literacy." *Reading Research Quarterly* 21 (1986): 360–406.

_____. "Romance and Reason." *The Reading Teacher* 47 (1994): 280–291.

Treiman, R. *Beginning to Spell: A Study of First-Grade Children.* Oxford University Press, 1993.

Yopp, H. K. "Developing Phonemic Awareness in Young Children." *The Reading Teacher* 45 (1992): 696–703.

Bibliography of Classroom Resource Materials

Allen, M. *Dr. Maggie's Play and Discover: Phonics.* Creative Teaching Press, 1998.

Bear, D. B., M. Invernizzi, and S. Templeton. *Words Their Way: A Developmental Approach to Phonics, Spelling, and Vocabulary.* Macmillan/Merrill, 1995.

Cunningham, P., and D. P. Hall. *Phonics They Use: Words for Reading and Writing.* 2d ed. HarperCollins, 1995.

Erickson, R. *The Amazing Alphabet Puppets.* Creative Teaching Press, 1995.

Fitzpatrick, J. *Phonemic Awareness: Playing with Sounds to Strengthen Beginning Reading Skills.* Creative Teaching Press, 1997.

_____. *Reading Strategies That Work! Helping Young Readers Develop Independent Reading Skills.* Creative Teaching Press, 1998.

Fry, E. *How to Teach Reading: For Teachers, Parents, and Tutors.* Laguna Beach Educational Books, 1995.

_____. *Phonics Patterns: Onset and Rhyme Word Lists.* Laguna Beach Educational Books, 1994.

Hill, S. *Developing Literacy Using Reading Manipulatives.* Creative Teaching Press, 1997.

Holliman, L. *The Complete Guide to Classroom Centers.* Creative Teaching Press, 1996.

Jordano, K., and T. Callella-Jones. *Fall Phonemic Awareness Songs & Rhymes.* Creative Teaching Press, 1998.

_____. *Spring Phonemic Awareness Songs & Rhymes.* Creative Teaching Press, 1998.

_____. *Winter Phonemic Awareness Songs & Rhymes.* Creative Teaching Press, 1998.

Kurth, M. *Pocket Chart Alphabet Activities.* Creative Teaching Press, 1996.

McCracken, R., and M. McCracken. *Songs, Stories, and Poetry to Teach Reading and Writing.* Peguis, 1988.

Traugh, S. *Fun Phonics.* Creative Teaching Press, 1993.